FAMILY NIGHTS

STORIES TO MAKE YOU SMILE, AND INSPIRE YOU TO SEE THE HUMOR IN OUR
MONDAY NIGHT TRADITION FROM MORMONS YOU KNOW AND LOVE.

Compiled by

ANNE BRADSHAW

CFI
Springville, Utah

© 2009 Anne Bradshaw

ISBN 13: 978-1-59955-292-7

Published by CFI, an imprint of Cedar Fort, Inc., 2373 W. 700 S., Springville, UT 84663
Distributed by Cedar Fort, Inc. www.cedarfort.com

LIBRARY OF CONGRESS CATALOGING-IN-PUBLICATION DATA

Famous family nights / compiled by Anne Bradshaw.
    p. cm.
  ISBN 978-1-59955-292-7 (acid-free paper)
  1. Family home evenings (Mormon Church)--Anecdotes. 2. Mormon
families--Anecdotes. 3. Family--Religious life--Anecdotes. I. Bradshaw,
Anne Christine. II. Title.

  BX8643.F3F37 2009
  249.088'289332--dc22

2009009920

Cover design by Jen Boss
Cover design © 2009 by Lyle Mortimer
Edited and typeset by Melissa J. Caldwell

Printed in the United States of America

10 9 8 7 6 5 4 3 2 1

Printed on acid-free paper

For many cherished friends in England and the U.S. who helped our family grow in countless ways. May your home evenings bring you happiness and keep you grounded in the gospel of Jesus Christ.

Contents

★ ★ ✦ ★ ★

Acknowledgments

W HEN I BEGAN GATHERING MATERIAL FOR THIS book, I wasn't fully aware how many talented LDS people were prominent in their professions across the world. Those highlighted here are but a fraction of the actual number. I'm grateful to all participants for their helpful and kind responses, their cheers and encouragement that kept me going over humps and dips. I now also value email more than ever before. *Famous Family Nights* would have taken years to complete without it.

Appreciation goes to Cedar Fort, Inc. who saw something good in this book—something that could entertain, inform, and encourage us all to make family night work.

I particularly want to recognize LDStorymaker friends and other colleagues who prodded me when quitting seemed like a more comfortable option, and helped me fathom the mysteries of making a trailer to market this book. Author friend C. S. Bezas deserves a special tribute for kindly sharing her excellent family home evening ideas on my website at www.annebradshaw.com.

Screenwriter Jeanne McKinney and my son Pete gave invaluable advice, as did Marsha Ward, J. Scott Savage, Lu Ann Staheli, Bruce Young, Tristi Pinkston, Ron Johnston, Marvin Perkins, and Randy Cutliff. And my husband, Bob, deserves an extra "thank you"—for putting up with more than the occasional baked beans on toast (a British treat) while I typed forever.

I'm indebted to all these good people, but none more so than Canada's talented song writer and musician, Sara Lyn Baril. Sara's composition "Make it Last" is the background music for this book's promotional video now playing on the Internet at www.annebradshaw.blogspot.com, YouTube, and other locations. Thank you, Sara, for sharing your talent.

Introduction

I RECALL MISSING A HOME EVENING HERE and there when our children were young, but more clearly do I remember good (and not-so-good) evenings when my husband and I pulled together and made things happen. Our children too made things happen—the good dominating with age and practice. At one stage, when chaos reigned more frequently than not, we laughed at one small son's name for home evening. He couldn't quite say the long title, so he shortened it to "foam evening." It was years before he knew that his long-suffering parents pictured themselves foaming at the mouth when they smiled, copied him, and called out, "Time for foam evening."

Families can bond with each other and with the Savior during family home evening. As both a parent and writer, I lend my commitment to this ideal by joining other LDS individuals, including those who work as artists, writers, sports leaders, and professionals in many fields. Together, we stand strong and raise our voices that all might rekindle enthusiasm and determination to follow the prophet's plea— that we consistently hold family home evening.

After all, what do we take with us to heaven? Family. Invest in no-fail, low-risk, wealth-building stocks and bonds that Wall Street cannot plunder—the family.

Family home evening is difficult to accomplish because it really does cement loving relationships. This makes it a number-one target for the adversary. On the one hand, clear instructions from Church leaders suggest setting aside Monday night for this purpose. On the other hand, opposition in its many seemingly innocent, yet compelling, disguises says "quit because it's not worth the effort."

President James E. Faust explains how very much "worth the effort" home evening is when he says, "Devotion to God developed in family home evening seems to forge the spiritual moorings and stability that can help families and individuals cope with the complexities of life."[1]

For some reason, digging up new potatoes in the dark from our English garden stands out in my family's memory as a successful home evening that forged this kind of stability. Maybe it was because we saw the fruits of earlier labors. However, less memorable lessons must have also borne fruit, because most of those same children now hold their own family nights.

I'm grateful for all the wonderful contributors to this book. Their experiences are as diverse as the occupations for which they are known. In addition to following the *Family Home Evening Resource Book,* the new *Behold Your Little Ones,* and using the scriptures and Church magazines, each family has prayerfully developed ideas to meet its needs. The results may spark concepts readers can adapt for personal use.

President Gordon B. Hinckley wrote an article for the *Ensign* titled, "Family Home Evening." In it, he expressed growing concern that the family home evening program was fading. He said,

> Brethren, there is nothing more important than your families. You know that. This program was begun back in 1915, 87 years ago, when President Joseph F. Smith urged the Latter-day Saints to set aside one evening a week devoted specifically to the family. It was to be a time of teaching, of reading the scriptures, of cultivating talents, of discussing family matters. It was not to be a time to attend athletic events or anything of the kind. Of course, if there is family activity of such a kind occasionally, that may be all right. But in the increasingly frantic rush of our lives, it is so important that fathers and mothers sit down with their children, pray together, instruct them in the ways of the Lord, consider their family problems, and let the children express their talents. I am satisfied that this program came under the revelations of the Lord in response to a need among the families of the Church.[2]

It is never too late to begin. Married or single, with or without children, all can benefit. There is no guarantee, of course, that all will stay close to the gospel. Each child of God has agency, and some spirits will choose to wander. But when families build upon strong foundations, opportunities to achieve cherished eternal goals greatly increase.

So please, read on, and enjoy the variety of stories and the theme running through this book—that families are precious, challenging, and worth every ounce of effort to strengthen in the gospel of Jesus Christ. Home evening is a priceless tool that can help achieve family harmony and nurture testimonies of the Savior.

In these pages, you will find not only great lesson and activity ideas, but also hope, comfort, and humor to get you through all your "foam evenings."

NOTES

1. James E. Faust, "Enriching Our Lives through Family Home Evening," *Ensign,* June 2003, 2–6.

2. Gordon B. Hinckley, "Family Home Evening," *Ensign,* Mar. 2003, 2–5.

Traci Hunter Abramson *spent years working for the U.S. Central Intelligence Agency. She is the Whitney Award-winning author of several LDS suspense novels including,* The Deep End, Freefall, Royal Target, *and* Lockdown.

Do You Have Anything to Bring Up?

I WASN'T RAISED IN THE CHURCH, so family home evening was new to me as a parent. I observed how other families faced different challenges when trying to meet together each Monday night. My family was falling prey to these common problems when several conference talks addressed the importance of holding family home evening. I took the words of our leaders to heart. My husband and I started with simple activities on Monday nights, usually in the form of a family game. We loved interacting with our kids this way and realized it was important for every member of the family to learn how to be a good loser as well as a good winner.

As our older children became teenagers, my husband started asking a simple question at the beginning of each family home evening: "Do you have anything to bring up?" Answers to this weekly question helped mold our family. Comments often included simple issues of respect and compatibility and the inevitable requests for allowance. Other times, issues of greater importance were raised, including everything from how to help family members with serious medical problems to choosing a name for our youngest child. Following these discussions, our family enjoyed a family game—something that spilled over into other occasions, especially during hurricane season when we often lose our power. Games are as much a part of our emergency supplies as are the battery-powered lanterns.

Several months ago when I was at a school event with my youngest daughter, a tornado warning was issued. Everyone was instructed to move into the hallways for safety. Knowing that my teenagers were home with my youngest child, I flipped open my cell phone as my daughter and I moved into the hallway with everyone else.

My oldest daughter answered the phone in her usual cheerful manner. I told her about the tornado warning and suggested that she go down to the basement and watch television with her brother and sister until the threat had passed. She let out a little laugh as she informed me they were already in the basement and she would see me when I got home.

I continued into the hallway where a friend, who was also a teacher at the school, stopped me. She was clearly amused and took time to explain why. Apparently, the vast majority of people at the school had shifted into panic mode as I made my casual phone call to my daughter. The daughter who was with me showed no signs of stress, and no one in my family seemed the least bit concerned about the tornado sighted in our area.

In the hallway, we sat next to another woman and her daughter who attended the same ward at church. This friend was equally calm despite the fact that five of her children were also home alone. Then it hit me. We didn't need to panic. Not only did we have faith that the Lord would watch over our families, but we also had confidence our children knew what to do in an emergency. They hadn't been given just one lesson on how to survive a natural disaster; they had received many. Every week, they bonded and connected with other family members and absorbed an understanding of what to expect from us as parents as well as what to expect from each other.

The tornado didn't touch down that night. I did however gain a new insight. Through simple obedience, my family was prepared for the unexpected in ways I never could have anticipated. All these blessings resulted from starting a home evening conversation with a simple question: "Do you have anything to bring up?"

Linda Paulson Adams *is the author of two LDS novels*—Prodigal Journey *and* Refining Fire. *Linda also works as a freelance editor, public speaker, singer, and songwriter.*

★ ★ Just Do It! ★ ★

FAMILY HOME EVENINGS IN OUR HOME RANGE from the well-planned and organized, to the more frequent "What are we doing tonight? Eeek, it's 7:30!" variety. The most critical thing is to hold the meeting: ready or not, here it comes! Just do it!

We have a variety of ages to keep interested, which is a challenge. As lifetime LDS parents, we're well-schooled in the ideal FHE routine: opening and closing songs perfectly matched to well thought-out lessons, accompanied by interesting visual aids, during which all the children are reverent and participate in a lovely gospel discussion. No one is running amok with underwear on their head, calling out inappropriate answers, or poking their sibling with some pointy object. Every so often, we hit pay dirt and get one of those cool, ideal evenings where the Spirit is profoundly present. It's a beautiful thing when it happens.

But we have real children—a lot of them—and try as we might, they don't all behave. And they don't all get along with each other all the time nor do they always want to be there. And any of you with teenagers knows the sound I call The Grunt. It's an answer, a shrug, a pledge of annoyance all at once. Hearing The Grunt during family home evening most likely elicits from one or both parents the innuendo that someone in the family is behaving like Laman and Lemuel, which accusation elicits yet another Grunt.

We find when we keep serious discussion to ten or fifteen minutes and bookend it with a little fun or nonsense, the kids hold their attention a little better—okay, a lot better—than when one or the other parent (or both) wax eloquent and complicate the simplicity of the gospel by inserting lots of words—in other words, lectures. Keeping it fun works.

Below are some ideas we've used for the "Eeek, it's 7:30!" home evenings.

- ★ Get everyone together in the same room. Have a prayer, and announce family Project Night. For the next hour, everyone gets out one of those UFO's (Un-Finished Objects) we all have lying around and works on it. Smaller children can color a picture or play quietly with a toy. Legos or other building toys work well. Expect older children to groan and complain at first, but when we've done this, amazingly, everyone is able to find something to do.

- ★ Get everyone together in front of the TV, have a prayer, and then pop in a Church or seminary video or conference talk. You can subscribe to a set of General Conference DVDs delivered to your home the same way you order Church magazines. Many Church videos are available for low prices from the Church distribution center at www.ldscatalog.org.

- ★ Get everyone together in front of the piano, have a prayer, and have a family sing-along. Hymns and Primary songs are ideal, but hey, if you're having fun jamming to Come Sail Away, or Girls Camp songs, why not? You're together. And sharing talents. I was afraid one-third of my kids would revolt when we tried this one, but we had a blast, and even The Grunts had disappeared by the end.

The point is to stick together and stick to it. Once the family know you mean business, and that they are not getting out of this family time, they might even start to enjoy it.

Michael Allred *is a comic book artist &
writer, screenwriter, filmmaker, producer, actor,
guitarist, vocalist, former European television
reporter, and creator of many comic book sensa-
tions, including* Madman, *and the* Red Rocket
7 *series. Mike has worked on most major comic
book character, including* Batman, Superman,
and Spider-man. *His most recent work,* The
Golden Plates, *is an adaptation of* The Book of
Mormon.

★ ★ Sharing Home Evening ★ ★

M Y WIFE, LAURA, AND I NOTICED THAT our kids always loved the
missionaries, so some of our best family nights have been when
we invited missionaries for dinner and then tied the visit into family
home evening. This always provides freshness, focus, and energy, and
helps the kids get more involved.

The most unique evening by far was what happened after I went
with the missionaries to visit "soft contacts." I met a young lady who
was investigating the church, so I invited her to our home for family
night, telling her we had a son her age. Long story short, they couldn't
take their eyes off each other and ended up getting married. A year
after her baptism, they were sealed in the Portland temple.

Favorite memories are filled with times we shared family night
with others, such as with our friend Sister Wendy Trent singing and
playing the piano. In my childhood, we also made crunchy crepes and
filled them with our choice of pudding. I remember, not just because
the crepes were tasty, but also because of the fun we had making them
and eating them together. Sharing time, talents, and the gospel with
others is always a powerful and positive way to go.

Michele Wood Baer *has been a solo-ist and has directed choirs in Utah, California, Connecticut, and Arizona. Mother of six children and grandmother of two grandchildren, she was honored as the American Mothers National Vocal Winner in 2003 and has recorded three vocal CDs of inspirational music, including* Never Give Up: Songs of Faith and Family. *She is currently a presenter at Especially For Youth and the state director of the Family Leader Network in Arizona.*

★ ★ Generations of Family ★ ★ Home Evenings

MY PARENTS WERE STALWART IN THE GOSPEL of Jesus Christ and taught me by example how to live it. They also followed the prophet's counsel to have "regular family home evenings." So we did, each Monday night. Some lessons have blurred with time, but the picture I have of sitting on the couch having dialogue, sometimes heated, with my siblings, stays etched in my mind. It is a nuclear family memory—the feeling we were one and all there together—no empty chairs.

Of course, I don't mean to mislead. Family nights were not perfect kids sitting quietly listening to counsel from their parents each week. It was sometimes resisted togetherness! I know that one lesson I gave in my early teens was well prepared but ended up bringing me to tears since, "Nobody would be quiet and listen to the lesson!"

It seems everyone thinks what they have to say is the most impor-tant. But then, isn't that the genius of FHE? All members feeling they have valued input and a place to share it? The closeness we seven siblings continue to feel, some forty years later, is testament to the diligence our parents took in gathering us each week for gospel instruction.

Now of course you have to know we had fun activities too. There was the tradition of making homemade root beer with a large garbage can, extract, bottle canner, and a keg in which it all fermented. The assembly line was a blast. We also made a hard taffy recipe called honey candy that each got to pull with buttered hands until it cooled. We kept eating it through the following week.

Games were a big part of home evening, and with healthy competition going in our family, we sometimes had to end the games early! "Slapsies, Creepsies Crawlsies" was a great favorite that involved hiding a fifty-cent piece across the table from the other team. Team A started by passing a fifty-cent piece back and forth in their hands under the table until team B said "stop." Then all players on team A raised closed fists and rested their elbows on the table. Team B told Team A to do one of actions: Slapsies—slap their hands on the table on the count of three, leaving team B to guess which hand had the coin. Or Creepsies Crawlsies—they carefully slid closed fists up over the edge of the table, slowly moving their open hands, palms down to rest on the table, again leaving team B to guess which hand had the coin. The points of each round were counted by how many hands it took to find the coin. Then the coin switched sides and the other team had a turn to pass it, and so on.

With my own family of six children, I have continued to hold family home evenings. It is sometimes hard to start, but setting a consistent time helps. As soon as we start playing the hymn, all gather and a great spirit enters our home. I know the children feel it too as we sing because at first they resist, but by the end of all the verses, we have full blown four-part harmony (okay, we do have a musical family). By then it is easier to get cooperation, shared planning, and learning because we are together in a spirit of love. Some of the lessons have great visual aids while others are gospel discussions. Relationships become stronger because of this time investment and open communication.

All families have the potential to improve and all families can build ties that grow stronger and bring greater peace and comfort. Family home evening is an inspired program to assist us in this great endeavor.

Shirley Bahlmann *is the author of thirteen books including* Life Is like Riding a Unicycle *and* Friends From Beyond the Veil. *She is also known for her collections of historical pioneer stories such as* The Pioneers: A Course in Miracles, *and the Odd series.*

 # Bring on the Laundry

THE FAMILY HOME EVENINGS OF MY CHILDHOOD usually consisted of Dad calling his eight children several times to "come to home evening" before we actually assembled in the living room. We slouched on the couch unless my little sister, Bev, got there first. Wrapped in a crocheted afghan, she lay prone on the couch cushions, forcing some of us to find seats on the floor. The lessons were always from the home evening manual and varied in length from five minutes to fifty, depending on who gave it.

The treats ranged from graham crackers handed around straight from the box to Baked Alaska, depending on who drew the treat assignment. The activity could range from watching the circus on TV to folding laundry, which wasn't as boring as you may think, especially with Bev there. One time, she broke us up into peals of laughter when she put a pair of underpants on her head and pulled her pigtails through the leg holes. My brother countered by stuffing his legs into the long sleeves of a button-up shirt and sliding his arms into a pair of jeans, and then moving around the room like a clown walking upside down. I laughed so hard I could barely breathe. Then everyone got into the act, putting on clean clothes that weren't theirs in the weirdest combinations they could think of. Mom didn't tell us to stop. After the activity, the closing prayer for home evening was our family nighttime prayer, and it was always brief.

I'm sure I learned subliminal life lessons from my childhood home evenings. My current family has adapted somewhat from years gone by. We hold home evening on Sunday night. Sometimes we have an activity on Monday, depending on work schedules. Sometimes, we draw lessons from places outside the manual, such as Seminary or Primary. One memorable lesson given by our teenager was about crunching people's chips. He took a snack sized potato chip bag and smashed it with his hand repeatedly, saying mean things to the potato chips, like, "You're so greasy!" "I hate you!" "You belong in the garbage can!" "You're stale, stale, stale!" I had to wonder about his sanity until he held up the bag and said, "It still looks normal, doesn't it?" The bag hadn't split, and it indeed looked normal. Then he popped open the top and showed us the crumbs inside. "But on the inside, it's all smashed up," he explained. "That's like people. If you aren't nice to them, they get all smashed up inside, even though you can't see it."

Most recently, our Primary-aged son Michael saw a Sharing Time that involved handing individual children baggies containing a single ingredient, such as a raw egg, baking chocolate, a teaspoon of salt, a bit of baking powder, flour, or shortening. The children with the baggies were told that they had a wonderful treat, and they could go ahead and eat it. No one did. The lesson culminated with the idea that when everything is mixed together (when everyone helps one another) it makes a delicious treat. (It turned out to be chocolate chip cookies that everyone got to eat.)

It is harder to get people together for home evening when ages range from a teenager to an eight-year-old. Our home evenings may be hit and miss, but I feel the importance of holding them as much as I feel hunger for good nutrition. Hey, I just had an idea for our next family night . . . bring on the clean laundry! I feel like dressing up.

Sara Lyn Baril, *from Alberta, Canada, writes inspirational songs, choir numbers, children's music, and country and love songs. She composed eleven songs for a stake play, entitled* Finding My Way, *performed under her musical direction by the Saskatoon, Saskatchewan Stake. She also wrote music for a Christmas cantata,* Glorious Is His Name, *performed in Raymond (1999) and in Saskatoon (2004), and for the Sounds of Zion Concert Tour in Canada, 2007. Her debut CD,* Thy Healing Hands—Songs of Comfort and Peace, *is produced by Greg Hansen.*

★ ★ Power in Gathering ★ ★

WHEN I WAS GROWING UP, FAMILY HOME evening was a time we reserved just for us. On Monday nights, the phone went off the hook and we were expected to be home—by six o'clock. I don't recall every lesson or every activity (although weeding the garden was sometimes disguised as FHE), but I do recall that it was something we did . . . most of the time—and we always had a treat afterward.

With eight kids going eight different directions five nights a week, I commend my parents for the efforts they made. They weren't perfect, but they tried. Regardless of the quality of our family home evenings, I gained an appreciation for my family, parents, and my heritage, and gained a testimony of various gospel topics. Following the prophet by having weekly home evening was a powerful lesson in itself that taught us it was more important than whatever we were doing, and that following a prophet's counsel was worth the sacrifice.

I learned over the last few years that FHE doesn't always run exactly like the manual. Life is busy! But we can still gather each week for something. Through my own experience now, as a mother of five children under age ten and in the thick of reality, I have learned:

1. If the prophet says to do it—do it. Blessings will come!
2. There is help for FHE! There are so many great resources the church provides; Preach My Gospel, Family Home Evening Resource Book, Behold Your Little Ones, and Church magazines.

In addition, countless places on the internet have FHE ideas.

3. Keep it simple. Long, preachy family nights never fly.

4. If FHE starts late, just read a story from the Friend or a scripture story, or something out of great-grandfather's journal. Start it with a song and prayer, and end with family prayer. There is power in gathering (Matthew 18:20).

5. To disguise gardening or attending brother's baseball game as FHE is okay sometimes. Although it is ideal to include a lesson with each FHE, it's the getting together that counts. Again, there is power in gathering.

6. Be adaptable. Babies will cry, toddlers will have had enough five minutes into the lesson, teenagers have homework and projects, and sometimes the realities of family life often require adaptations to family night.

7. Have fun! Like the FHE song says: "When the family gets together after evening work is done, then we learn to love each other, popping corn and having fun."[1] Creating happy memories will strengthen the family.

8. Remember that the Atonement covers families too. All we are ever asked is to do our best. When we do that, the Lord can make up for inadequacies.

NOTE

1. "Family Night," *Children's Songbook* (Salt Lake City: The Church of Jesus Christ of Latter-day Saints, 1989), 194.

Larry Barkdull *is a longtime publisher and writer of books, music, art, and maga-zines. He published the* Tabernacle Choir Performance Library *and over 600 prod-ucts for numerous authors, composers and art-ists. He founded two non-profit organizations to advance LDS arts and to promote the gospel of Jesus Christ on the Internet. His books have won various awards: American Family Best Fic-tion Award; Benjamin Franklin Book Award; and the Book of the Year Award from* Fore-word Magazine. *Larry is also the author of a new major work entitled* The Three Pillars of Zion.

★ ★ Temple Impression ★ ★

FROM THE OUTSET OF OUR MARRIAGE, BUFFIE and I held family home evening. When the children were small—and we have ten of them!—the lessons often revolved around the theme of being nice to each other. When the children became teenagers, the themes often revolved around being nice to Mom and Dad! Of course, we took turns with lessons, studied the scriptures, sang songs, and ended with treats, which kept everyone still for the duration.

Although some people in our ward called it family hour, we were lucky to stretch it out to thirty minutes. We always faced the chal-lenge of subjects—either they went over the heads of the young ones, or they seemed too juvenile for the older ones. If we did not achieve quality, we at least attained quantity. And maybe that was enough. We certainly would never have made the cover of the Ensign as the model family for family home evening, but somehow we made it work, and remarkably, the kids look back on those times with fondness.

As a young father, I erroneously imagined the day when the chil-dren would be gone and family home evenings would pass to the next generation. That is, until I went to the temple one day and learned otherwise. The message was clear. I had not received a release. I was still Dad, and as the patriarch of this large and growing family, I had a responsibility to teach my adult children the gospel. When my wife and I discussed the options, we both came to the conclusion that despite the logistical challenges—gathering together thirty-two people into one house on the same day, arranging for babysitters, and so forth—we had to move forward to make it work.

Here is what we decided: She and I would be the primary teachers. This was Mom and Dad's family home evening. We would meet on Fast Sundays and rotate babysitters. We would film the lesson for those who could not join, and also to review. I would write a detailed lesson, which the children would put into a binder for future reference.

Remarkably, it worked, and everyone loved it. We dug into gospel subjects talked about things like "The Proper Way to Study the Scriptures," "Who We Really Are," "Financial Planning Basics," and "God's Attributes and Characteristics." When our son went on a mission, we sent him audio tapes of our family home evenings. Our gospel literacy increased, as did our family unity. Our discussions led to subsequent discussions, and we learned that our children used the principles that we talked about in lessons in their home wards. Perhaps the greatest benefit was the opportunity that my wife and I had to bear our testimonies. Consequently, our children cannot doubt what we believe and how deeply we believe it. They know that we love the Lord, we love each other, and we love each of them. They know that we value our sealing above every other consideration, and they know that our sealing tethers them to us with unbreakable cords of eternal love.

And this all started with an impression in the temple.

Dallyn Vail Bayles, *an actor, singer, and recording artist (solo album,* Prayer*), has performed throughout the U.S. and Canada in the Broadway touring companies of* The Phantom of the Opera *and* Les Misérables. *He has roles in many Church movies, including that of Hyrum Smith in both* Joseph Smith: The Prophet of the Restoration *and* Emma Smith: My Story, *and leads in three* Liken the Scriptures *films. Dallyn took lead roles in* The Light of the World *and* Savior of the World, *and featured as guest soloist with the Mormon Tabernacle Choir on Music and the Spoken Word.*

★ ★ Lessons Learned ★ ★

ONE SUNDAY AFTER CHURCH, OUR FIVE-YEAR-OLD DAUGHTER, Audrey, told me what she'd learned that day in Primary concerning a simple principle of the gospel. My wife, Rachel, and I were so impressed with what Audrey remembered from the Primary lesson, including stories and presentation ideas, that it occurred to us this would be a perfect family home evening lesson, so I asked her to share it with us the next day.

Audrey went to work drawing pictures showing members of our family applying this principle and getting out her stuffed animals and dolls to rehearse a story of her own making with characters who needed to learn this principle. Her lesson was marvelous! It was spiritual, beautiful, imaginative, and simple in its presentation—just like a child. I could not have been prouder of my little girl as I watched her teach me principles of the gospel of Jesus Christ that we all needed to learn. There were plenty of "melt-your-heart" moments.

Not only did Audrey enjoy herself and become excited about home evening, but it also inspired her younger brother to want to share lessons. Warner, our shyer child, got out of his comfort zone and started teaching simple gospel principles in his own wonderful way. Our children now look forward to family night and their chance to participate. We feel it has truly brought us closer together.

These experiences made me think of the saying that if you want someone to learn a principle well, have them teach it to someone else. Up to that point, I assumed my wife and I would present lessons until the children were older, had a better understanding of gospel principles, and had better organizational and presentation skills. I was very wrong. Our children understood these principles already and could present lessons in a phenomenal way.

Rachel and I will sometimes tell them to prepare a lesson on a particular topic that we feel we need to learn as a family, but most of the time we let them choose the topic. This simple decision to have the children teach has made a huge difference. "Out of the mouths of babes" and "a little child shall lead them" can be real experiences, especially in home evening. We used to think we had to give full-scale lessons with visual aids and other complicated preparations. We now realize simplicity is important no matter what the age.

We will soon have to deal with a new set of challenges in holding our regular home evenings. I will be joining the tour of *The Phantom of the Opera*. This means I will be away from my family for at least a month at a time between tour stops. During this continuous separation, we plan to utilize the great blessing of technology and have FHE together via video conferencing. We also plan to do this for our family prayers each day. No matter what our circumstances may be, we can adjust and make it work. Sometimes you have to adjust from the norm and the ideal to make it work. You may have to change the day you hold family night, its duration, and even the method, but the important thing is to make sure you have it consistently. Our family has definitely been blessed and brought closer together by following this guideline.

Julie Coulter Bellon *is a Canadian writer of four LDS Romantic Suspense novels, including* Time Will Tell, *and* All's Fair. *She also teaches at BYU and is author of the best seller* Be Prepared: A Parent's Guide to Boy Scouts and the Duty to God Award—What You Should Know.

★ ★ Mists of Darkness ★ ★

WHEN MY CHILDREN WERE YOUNG, FAMILY HOME evening was hard. My husband and I would prepare lessons and try to involve the children, but it seemed like they had saved up all of their arguing and teasing for Monday night, and nothing we said or did seemed to change that. One Monday afternoon, I was particularly discouraged. I was sitting on my porch steps when I should have been inside starting dinner and getting ready for family night. My oldest son, who was five at the time, joined me on the steps and just as I was going to go inside, we saw that there was a fire a block or two away at our local greenhouse. The thick dark smoke quickly rose in the sky as the plastic sheeting started to burn, and with the slight breeze that was present, the smoke billowed toward our home. My son and I stood watching the fire when he suddenly turned to me and pointed at the black smoke and said, "Look Mom, the mists of darkness are coming." It was a small comment, but in that moment I knew some teaching was getting through the haze of arguments and teasing. He had listened! He knew about the mists of darkness. I don't think I could keep the smile off of my face for the rest of that day.

Soon after, I started making up family nights for our young children that had a game relating to a gospel principle. For example, we would tape a sign to one child's chest that read, "Eternal Happiness," and then we would have the child hide. We would all seek for him and then talk about how we are searching for eternal happiness and what we have to do to find it. Or we would draw the word SIN in large chalk letters on our driveway and let the children draw pictures all around it. Then we would talk about how sin makes marks on our souls, just like we made marks on the driveway. As we washed the chalk away with the hose, we talked about how Jesus Christ washes away our sins as well. It was these home evenings in which everyone participated that seemed to make the arguing stop as we focused instead on what was taught.

As the children grew older, we kept up the tradition of everyone participating. One of our favorite family nights is when we make a laminated 8½ x 11-inch ward list with the names, addresses, and phone numbers on one side and a ward map on the other and give those out as a Christmas gift to our ward. The kids always have a favorite teacher or neighbor with whom they want to share. It's also a nice thing to have when new neighbors move in, so we can go and greet them throughout the year. We make the list a bright color so it's never lost in a pile of paper, and do different colors for each year to include any changes that may have occurred. We also put a magnet on the back so it can be magnetized to the refrigerator. That way it's always handy! It's a great way of getting to know our neighbors as well as spending time together as a family doing a service for the ward family.

Doing family nights regularly, even when it was hard, has really helped me know my children better and build a foundation of gospel principles to help them in their lives. Now I look forward to Monday evening because even though there is still an occasional argument, I know they're listening and that we will be blessed for our efforts.

C. S. Bezas *owns LDSMusicals.org, a site for free LDS stage productions and music. In addition, she writes for* Meridian Magazine, *and is the editor for* BellaOnline. *A keynote speaker across the U.S., she has also performed on television, stage, and film, including an appearance as Anne Frank with the Florida Orchestra. Her latest book is* Powerful Tips for Powerful Teachers.

★ ★ That Awkward Family ★ ★ Home Evening

A S A KID, I WAS NOT FAMILIAR with the concept of family home evening. We were a busy family and had not yet found the Mormon faith or the phrase FHE. Flash forward a few years, and my parents were soon struggling with implementing this strange new tradition. I remember the awkward early moments. As a young girl, it was hard to sit during lessons that felt foreign. My family had always had family vacations, outings, and other fun activities. But this new formal and spiritual approach to family—spiritual togetherness—felt strangely angular and uncomfortable.

I am not sure we ever did get FHE "right," but now that I'm an adult, I see the value of the effort, and the concept of family home evening feels far less awkward and more blessed.

My own children look forward to our time together on Monday nights. But my husband and I have worked to encourage this. I have found the more we as adults ensure the children's comfort (both physical and emotional), the more we all benefit thereby. We very much want to avoid "brow beating" our kids because of chastisement or punishment that came as a result of FHE! Children do desire to learn. They desire to be good. They generally want to please their parents. But their squirmy little bodies make those desires difficult to achieve sometimes.

We start with a song and an opening prayer (petitioning the Lord for aid is a powerful tool to successful family home evenings), and then ask for sharing of scriptural verses. The kids race to find and share a verse they read during the previous week. We found when the kids are sharing the message, they listen better to its meaning!

We then open up our time to a simple family game, such as "Duck, Duck Goose" or any other zany activity. By getting bodies moving (even the teens) and people laughing, we create memories. And at the end of the game, we tie it, or the activity, into a gospel principle pulled from the scriptures or from the For the Strength of Youth pamphlet.

One activity we chose turned out to be tremendously popular. We blindfolded our youngest child and asked him to follow his daddy's voice. His daddy would call out instructions to help our small son find him. The others in the room called out unhelpful advice. When our son finally "found" his father, he could remove the blindfold. Our son loved this activity and asked to play it repeatedly, entranced by the physical metaphor of the Lord versus the adversary.

After several repetitions, we allowed others to take turns. Even our oldest teen had fun playing the game. When done, we asked the kids to find a scripture verse they thought symbolized the activity. It was amazing to see what they found all on their own! As they took turns reading their verses and teaching the principle they felt those verses contained, we saw they were teaching themselves as well, and better yet, were immersing themselves in the activity!

My parents could not have foreseen the legacy they were leaving by attempting the awkward new concept of family home evening. I feel immense gratitude to them for the great benefit to my children and future posterity.

Christopher Kimball Bigelow *is the author of five books including* Mormonism for Dummies. *His novel* Kindred Spirits *was adopted as a textbook for a course on Mormonism at Massachusetts College of the Holy Cross. Chris co-founded and edited* The Sugar Beet, *and* Irreantum.

★ ★ Good Things and Bad Things ★ ★

MY WIFE AND I START FAMILY HOME evenings informally during dinner with a conversation game we call "Good Things and Bad Things." We go around the table and share the best and worst things that happened during the week. If someone is slow to answer, we move to the next. The kids enjoy being in the spotlight and helping each other think of events to report. By the time dinner is over, we're already into the home evening groove. We move into the living room, have a brief gospel lesson, and then a song and prayer. Sometimes we have an activity and a treat.

Kids enjoy object lessons. For one lesson on how the Book of Mormon functions as another witness of Jesus Christ, we used two pieces of two-by-four and two nails. First, we hammered the pieces together with one nail, which represented the Bible. With one nail as a pivot point, it's possible to turn the pieces of wood in many different directions, like the hands of a clock. Twisting the pieces in different ways is what gives rise to different religions, we explained. If we want the pieces to stay truly aligned, we need a second nail to hold them in place, so we hammered in the second nail and explained how it represented the Book of Mormon, which acts as a second witness of Christ.

But sometimes, if all we do is "Good Things and Bad Things" during dinner on a Monday night, then hey, at least that's something! Family home evening was created for the family, not the family for family home evening.

Davis Bigelow *is a photographer and author from Canada. His new book,* Three Seconds On, Three Seconds Off, *shares adventures from his youth growing up on Pointer Island Lightstation, a tiny and remote lighthouse off the Canadian west coast.*

★ ★ Six Squirming Children in a Lighthouse ★ ★

I WAS JUST THREE YEARS OLD. THE year was 1963. I lived in a remote lighthouse, cut off from the rest of the world, solitary and often alone. My growing up years on Pointer Island Lightstation were eventful and rarely dull. Excitement hung in each breath of humid, salty air ,like thick fog on a damp spring morning. But as I look back in time, a deep and brooding sense of regret overshadows me. I possess a treasure trove of sharp memories yet there is one treasure noticeably absent from my cherished collection. It is family home evening.

Our list of excuses probably included all your favourites, but we had a few unique justifications of our own. Our family held weekly Sacrament Meeting, Sunday School, Primary, Priesthood Meeting, Young Men's and Young Women's. On our acre-and-a-half island, we were usually together anyway, trapped by location and circumstance. We didn't just have family home evenings; we had family home days and weeks! Why should we meet formally more often than we already did? And as if those reasons were not enough, when each of us six children grew older, we boarded with various families in far away places to attend school. When Christmas, Easter, or summer holidays arrived, we all scampered home. Our happy reunions were chock full of storytelling, game playing, movie watching, beach combing, fishing, boating, exploring the nearby woods, swimming in the summer, and cutting Christmas trees in the winter. Life was grand, and I knew no better—until I thought about it in 2008. Not once in my memories can I find one time when we did anything more than family activities as our substitute for a real family home evening. Other than church on Sunday, blessings on the food, family prayer, and personal prayer, we provided no opportunities for the Holy Ghost to shape our hearts.

As I consider the Davis Bigelow of today, I wonder what I might be like if I had been immersed in regular and fully functioning FHE. Among the weaknesses I still strive to overcome are items that very well could have been prevented by regular and proper family home evenings. For example, I have struggled for many years to overcome my "center-of-attention syndrome." I was never taught to let someone else shine as they presented a lesson, musical number, or talent. The endless games I enjoyed with my siblings and parents only served to teach me that the sharpest or the luckiest one could be the winner. I never cooperated in a service project, compromised with anyone, or had to share the spotlight. Properly structured family home evening could have taught me reverence for others, but alas, I was forced to learn that tough lesson later on in my life. My social skills, crippled by years in isolation, could have benefited greatly if I had been taught how to present lessons with the listeners in mind. I would have learned patience as I waited for my turn. I would have felt less alone and more like I was part of a team.

As you consider family home evening in your home, please realize that its potential benefits are gigantic! The implications are moral, social, spiritual, intellectual, and personal. The few minutes each week that you spend with your family could spell the difference between success and failure as a parent. Please don't sell yourself short. Make your FHE like a rich stew, not just nice tasting broth!

Dr. Susan Easton Black *joined the faculty of Brigham Young University in 1978 after receiving a bachelor's degree at BYU in Political Science, a master's degree from the University of California at San Bernardino in Counseling, and a doctorate degree from BYU in Educational Psychology. She is currently a professor of Church History and Doctrine and an Eliza R. Snow Fellow. She is a past Associate Dean of General Education and Honors and Director of Church History in the Religious Studies Center.*

Dr. Black has received numerous academic awards, including the Karl G. Maeser Distinguished Faculty Lecturer Award in 2000, and has authored, edited, and compiled over 100 books and 135 articles. Her most recent book is entitled Jesus Christ: Son of Man, King of Kings.

★ ★ It's Snowing ★ ★

"A s I Have Loved You, Love One Another" was the title of a family home evening lesson that changed the way my family viewed our neighbor, Mrs. Washburn. The lesson, like so many others, encouraged families to reach out in service and love to near neighbors. Just before the lesson ended, my youngest son, John, asked, "What about doing something nice for Mrs. Washburn?"

Wasel Washburn was the elderly widow who lived next door. She had raised ten children and was a grandmother to eighty-seven grandchildren. My first thought was, "Why Sister Washburn? She always has cars parked in front of her house filled with relatives who love and serve her. Surely, there is another neighbor that we could help."

However, in response to John's question, I asked my family, "Would you like to serve Sister Washburn?"

Brian answered, "I would like to pick a large bouquet of flowers from *her* garden and give them to her."

Catching the drift of his brother's plan, Todd said, "I would like to shovel her walks when it snows."

Since it was mid-August at the time, he presumed his service would be delayed, if not forgotten. When the laughter subsided, John said, "I will give her cookies."

Cookies were delivered and flowers picked, but Sister Washburn remained a neighbor, an associate, nothing more. She was someone we waved to if she happened to be outside as we hurried past.

Then came November, a change of weather, and a new dimension of friendship to our neighborhood. It began when I awoke to see a few inches of snow on the ground. "It snowed through the night," I said to Todd.

"I haven't waxed my skis. How could it have snowed already?" he replied.

"Before you think about skiing, what about shoveling Sister Washburn's walks?" I asked.

Todd moaned and said, "You remembered."

Yes, I had remembered and so had he. Todd got out of bed and reluctantly meandered outside.

To my surprise, he was back in the house in a few minutes. "I cannot possibly shovel her walks!" he said. "Sister Washburn has already done it."

I tried to imagine my elderly neighbor shoveling her walks, before saying, "I am so embarrassed. The whole family should have shoveled her walks."

With a big smile, Todd said, "You think you are embarrassed now—wait till you look out the window." As I looked, I saw Sister Washburn shoveling our walks.

In that act of charity, she was no longer just the woman who lived next door. Through the ensuing seventeen years, she was our dearest friend, confidant, and adopted grandmother. She called my sons, "Her boys." She died in August 1993 at the age of 96. Sister Washburn, farewell.

Jerry Borrowman *is the author of historical World War I and II novels,* 'Til The Boys Come Home, I'll Be Seeing You, As Time Goes By, Home Again At Last, *and* One Last Chance. *He has co-authored several biographies, including the award-winning* Three Against Hitler *with Rudi Wobbe.*

★ ★ Who Cleans Up the Game? ★ ★

W HEN OUR OLDEST CHILD WAS QUITE YOUNG, we decided to introduce him to board games. During one home evening, he came in last. Of course, the standard rule is that the loser cleans up the game. But he was so frustrated that he threw the game on the floor while making the heated assertion that he never wanted to play again.

As my wife and I talked about it later, we felt we had to do something to help the kids manage the inevitable frustration that comes with competition. Our prayers were answered in an unusual way, in that we were prompted to change the rules to where the winner has to clean up the game. That simple change made all the difference in the world and allowed us to play hundreds of games through the years with all our children.

Even now when they are all grown, we still find great joy in playing games with them and their spouses, whenever we get to together. It's interesting to predict, as the end of a game approaches and it becomes clear who is going to win, just who it is that will start the inevitable kidding of the winner that "Oh, well, it just means you have to clean up." Of course the winner doesn't mind, since they won. And the losers don't feel that insult is added to injury. Other families we've shared this with report it has brought increased serenity to their game nights as well.

As our children reached their teenage years, our oldest son started playing Scrabble with us every Sunday night. Eventually, his best friend joined in, soon making it a regular part of his life. Bless his heart, the young man simply couldn't spell. No matter, he often won, because he was an absolute genius at figuring out words that would cross double and triple tile squares.

After a few years of playing, this young man's parents started into the slow and painful process of divorce. Many were the nights when our Scrabble game became a haven of safety and emotional stability in his life. On a few occasions, because he'd learned to trust us, he and his sister came to our house to sleep, when things were particularly confrontational at their home.

The good news is that he grew into a great young man who fulfilled an honorable mission, married a terrific wife, and now is a kind and patient father. And, because of Scrabble, he learned to spell! Of far greater significance is that the social interaction of sitting around a table, chatting about life while contemplating a play fulfilled a vital need at a crucial time.

That's what makes family home evening board games so relevant, even in the modern world of electronic games. The unhurried pace of the game, the small table that brings people into face-to-face contact, and the fact that you have a game to cover a lull in the conversation, makes for a delightful hour or two outside the normal routines of life. Some of our best memories as a family come from the games we've played together, all around the world.

Anne Bradshaw *is an award-winning screenwriter and author of three books. She co-authored two writing self-help books and has countless published articles both online and in glossy magazines. Her compilation,* Please, No Zits! & Other Short Stories for LDS Youth, *can be used for family home evenings. Each story provides an opportunity for teenage/parent discussion.*

★ ★ Harmony—Most of the Time ★ ★

FAMILY HOME EVENINGS WERE SOMETHING MY HUSBAND, Bob, and I established early in our marriage, and they fast became a habit. If it hadn't been such an important and automatic thing to do each week while we had one young child, and then two, it would have been much more difficult to achieve by the time we had four independent youngsters growing more self-willed by the minute.

Our oldest son still remembers an FHE lesson when he was four. It was a simple, two minute presentation about being honest, and caused little David to feel instant guilt and confess to having cut down a bunch of daffodils in the next door neighbor's garden earlier that day. This prompted a chat about the steps of repentance, and Dave decided he would do something about it.

The next morning, Dave asked for some tomato plants from our garden, and then toddled off while I peeked and listened through the side window. After almost changing his mind a couple of times, he plucked up enough courage to knock on our neighbor's door. He explained where her daffodils went, presented his peace offering, and asked, "Will you forgive me?" Our neighbor's heart was touched, I experienced unexpected joy, and David never forgot the lesson he learned or the elation he felt afterward.

Another time, when two of our children went through a prickly stage, forever arguing over who owned what, we planned a short home evening lesson about harmony. We found two pictures. One showed children fighting over a toy, their faces scowling mad, one in tears. The other showed two children playing together, sharing a toy, smiles on their faces, eyes sparkling. The lesson was short, to the point, and included acting out scenes from the pictures. We were amazed to find our children understood. They were only age two and four, but they got it—for a week or two, anyway. We used those pictures many times when they needed reminding.

During teenage years, a home evening "special" was something we dubbed "Screen Test." These evenings were a good standby we used when schedules fell apart and life dumped excess baggage on us. But they were something each child remembers with good feelings of togetherness. Screen Test involved one person choosing his/her favorite TV program or video. As we watched, we all wrote questions relating to the story. While eating our treats, we took turns answering and discussing each other's questions. Bob and I guided the chat, and squeezed in gospel principles when possible. Another angle was reading a story from the New Era, followed by discussion.

We had our share of "Why-are-we-doing-this?" home evenings. But despite frustrations, feelings of inadequacy, and sometimes wishing we had kids who sat without a squeak or wriggle—despite all this, our memories are full and happy, and our family now pulls together with love, and yes, even harmony—most of the time.

RoseMarie Briggs *is executive director of the Family Leader Network. She worked as a syndicated radio reporter for more than 200 stations in the northwest and hosted a weekly radio program called "For Families." RoseMarie was an assistant scheduler for a U.S. Senate candidate and is a former marketing director for a top political technology company in Washington, D.C.*

★ ★ Was It Necessary? ★ ★

I CLEARLY REMEMBER AN IMPORTANT LESSON I learned when we had our first official family home evening. Our oldest children were two and three years old at the time. While saying the opening prayer, I had to hold back the tears because I felt the Spirit witness to me that I was doing the right thing and that family home evening was an inspired program. This was a powerful and life changing moment for me because I realized how important it was to be obedient to the Lord's specific counsel through his prophets.

I had not started home evenings earlier because I rationalized that as a stay-at-home mother of young children, we already had plenty of family time. It seemed as though about six out of seven nights a week my husband was home and all of us were together. I assumed we were already accomplishing the purpose of FHE, which is family togetherness. Yet, the Spirit helped me understand a very important lesson about doing things the Lord's way.

While family togetherness is obviously one purpose of family night, it is also about faith and obedience. Setting aside family time on Monday nights for a structured lesson and activity is something we've been advised to do for decades. As we follow that specific counsel, we are blessed.

My other children ages nine and ten enjoy giving the home evening lessons. My nine-year-old recently taught us about developing our talents. He used a story from the *Friend* about Spencer W. Kimball learning to play the piano. As a boy, President Kimball's father was concerned that young Spencer wasn't practicing the piano, so he made a deal with Spencer that if he would practice more, he could spend less time digging ditches. Spencer agreed and became a good piano player.

Later, when Spencer became a missionary, one of the ways he introduced himself at the door was to see if there was a piano in the front room. If there was a piano—especially a Kimball piano—he would say, "Would you like to hear a song on a Kimball from a Kimball?" Elder Kimball used playing hymns on the pianos of investigators to help bring the Spirit into the home and teach the gospel.

Both my nine- and ten-year-old have taken piano lessons for four years and regularly need nudging to keep up their practicing. All of us appreciated the story about President Kimball for two reasons. First, it showed that our talents can be used to help teach the gospel; and second, that even a boy who later grew up to be a prophet of God needed to be nudged to practice the piano!

Dr. Douglas Brinley *is a Family Life specialist with a Doctorate in Family Studies, and a Professor of Church History & Doctrine at Brigham Young University. He is the author of ten books, nine of which are on marriage and family relations, including best-selling book,* Between Husband and Wife. *He is a member of the AMCAP board and presents periodically on matters of marriage and marriage counseling to professional counselors.*

★ ★ Payoff Time ★ ★

I JUST RETIRED FROM FORTY-THREE YEARS OF teaching in Church Institutes and Religious Education at BYU Provo. Over the years I taught a class entitled, Teachings of the Living Prophets, a class where we studied conference talks and the words of living prophets. On one occasion I came across this statement: "It is one of the greatest blessings that God ever bestowed upon children that they have had parents who were in possession of true principles in relation to their Heavenly Father, salvation, eternal life, and were qualified and capable of teaching and traditionating their children in the same that they may be qualified to fulfill the object of their creation . . . . Ninety-nine out of every hundred children who are taught by their parents the principles of honesty and integrity, truth and virtue, will observe them through life."[1]

This last sentence was repeated by the First Presidency in five of the eight Family Home Evening manuals given to the Saints from 1965 to 1973. I liked the odds—ninety-nine out of a hundred children would "observe them through life." I decided I wanted that for my family. Family home evening was consistent in our home because of this promise as well as the obvious, practical blessings that come from regular time together in gospel discussions, playing together, and spending time with each other. I relied on that promise even if it didn't always appear that the kids knew of Pres. Woodruff's promise, as evidenced by this story my wife, Geri, tells:

31

My husband and I took turns teaching lessons until the children got older when we had them share in the opportunity. When it was Doug's turn, he usually taught something from the scriptures—more specifically—the Book of Mormon. He would start the lesson portion of the evening with an enthusiastic "Turn to chapter __" whatever chapter and verse he was focusing on that evening. "Now listen to this! These are the most exciting passages in the Book of Mormon!" or "This is my favorite chapter." He loved the Book of Mormon and his enthusiasm was evident. While all six of our children participated in FHE, we weren't always sure how much they absorbed. One son, Andy, always looked a little less interested than the rest. He rarely responded unless called upon and then with some effort to focus on our discussions.

However, the payoff came years later when he was serving a mission. He would write in his letters things like, "Dad, we were teaching this investigator and I heard myself saying, 'Just listen to this verse in the Book of Mormon! It is so important.' It came out of my mouth just like you always said it in FHE."

When we read that in his letter we looked at each other in amazement, laughed, and then appreciated President Woodruff's promise. Andy had been listening all along, but who would have guessed it at the time?

I think the point is that we do our best to teach our children, follow the counsel of living prophets, and we will be blessed. The Lord is aware of our efforts to bless His children too, for they are His as well.

NOTE

1. Wilford Woodruff, *Discourses of Wilford Woodruff,* ed. G. Homer Durham (Salt Lake City: Bookcraft, 1946), 266–68.

Laura M. Brotherson *is a marriage and family life educator and the author of a best-selling book on marital ONEness entitled,* And They Were Not Ashamed—Strengthening Marriage through Sexual Fulfillment. *Laura and her husband, Kevin, are the founders of Strengthening Marriage, Inc.*

This is the Night We've ★ ★ Waited For ★ ★

OF COURSE, THE FIRST THING MY KIDS said when I asked them what I should say about our family home evenings was that we have treats! There you have it! Apparently that's all you really need to know. They also said I should probably say something about the fact that we sing "Family Night" every single time we have family home evening. I've been a bit surprised that some people aren't familiar with this Primary song. I assumed it was a Mormon staple like, "I Am A Child of God."

> This the night we've waited for;
> Always a treat we have in store!
> We love each other more and more
> With ev'ry fam'ly night! [1]

Family home evening usually occurs on Monday nights in our house. We have a chart and take turns at conducting both the meeting and the music; saying the opening prayer; giving or choosing the lesson and/or activity; saying the closing family prayer; and being in charge of treats, which often ends up being little more than Graham Crackers and milk.

The kids told me to mention we also have family business each week where the person conducting asks each family member to report on anything they'd like to share about their day, their week, or their life. When it's Mommy's turn, she usually drags herself off the couch to review everything on the calendar for the coming week. That has really helped a lot to keep crisis management to a minimum with our family schedules. We make sure we note every basketball and dance practice, as well as scout meetings, activity days, dentist and orthodontist appointments, helping in kid's class times, date night, and church meetings. We really feel discombobulated if we miss doing this.

My favorite part of family home evening is when our kids give the lessons. We got a copy of the "Preach My Gospel" missionary manual for each of our children. It's pretty cool to see the amazing lessons pulled together for the family on topics such as the Holy Ghost, prayer, faith, repentance, humility, and baptism. Being the teacher is when we learn and internalize Gospel principles the most.

I love a quote from Joseph F. Smith and his counselors: "If the Saints obey this counsel to hold family home evening, we promise that great blessings will result. Love at home and obedience to parents will increase. Faith will be developed in the hearts of the youth of Israel, and they will gain power to combat the evil influences and temptations which beset them."[2]

Kids may see the family home evening treat as the most attractive feature of the night, but for parents it's obvious from the quote above that the family treat is so much more.

NOTES
1. *Children's Songbook,* 195.

2. Joseph F. Smith, "Family Home Evening," *Improvement Era,* June 1915, 734.

Matthew Buckley *(also known as Marion Jensen) is an author of children's and young adult books, including* Chickens in the Headlights *and* Bullies in the Headlights.

★ ★ We Tried—and Succeeded! ★ ★

HOME EVENING AT MY HOUSE WAS ALWAYS interesting. My parents had ten boys and one girl, and when you fit a crowd like that into a small living room, crazy things are bound to happen.

I remember sitting on the living room couch, examining the cover of the family home evening manual. A mother and father sat on a love seat. The father was dressed in a tie and was holding a picture; the mother wore a dress, a happy baby smiling on her lap. The room was immaculate. There was a picture of the temple above the couch, a glass-looking statue of the prophet on a side table, and a woven rug sprawled out on the floor.

On top of the rug were three happy children. The oldest boy looked strong and reliable; he sat with an elbow resting on his knee. A younger girl sat primly on the floor, looking in earnest at the picture and obviously paying attention to everything that was happening. Finally there was a smaller boy—the perfect younger brother. He sat with his hands in his lap.

And then there was the dog. A large, longhaired dog sat next to the younger boy, looking for all the world like he, too, was listening to what was going on. Here was a noble beast, protector against monsters or bears, whichever happened to come by in the dark of night.

What a reverent family—no wonder they had been chosen to be put on the cover of the Family Home Evening manual—the one I held close to my face as a shield, during our family nights. I didn't have safety goggles, so the manual served as the next best thing. I can picture in my mind what I would have seen if I'd lowered the manual, and peeked over the top.

My older brother has a set of Dad's old callipers and is measuring his own belly button lint. Two other brothers are wrestling over a soggy graham cracker stolen from the toddler. Another brother has fallen asleep and is drooling on Dad's shoulder.

Mom sighs. "So in conclusion, what is the topic of the lesson tonight?"

No response.

"I've mentioned it at least twenty times."

The noise level of the room seems to swell.

Mom looks around, sighs again, and then raises her voice to meet the clamor. "Can anybody tell me what one of the greatest sources of happiness is in this life?"

The answers come from everybody.

"Money!" "Food!" "TV!" "No, it's food."

"Aaaiigghh!"

I bet the kids on the manual would have known the answer. Probably even the dog could have enlightened us. But I've come to realize it's not all about that perfect setting. You'd be hard pressed to call our family home evenings "reverent." But we still learned, and drew closer as a family.

I think the name holds the secret. It's not church home evening, or reverent-time home evening. It's family home evening. I wouldn't trade those memories for anything on this earth.

Janet Burningham *is the author of two family home evening books,* Monday Nights in Zarahemla *and* Monday Nights in Nauvoo. *For several years, she worked as the Director of Education at the Sylvan Learning Center where she developed curriculum for various educational programs.*

It Really Does Make
★ ★ a Difference! ★ ★

I HAVE STRUGGLED WITH FAMILY NIGHT OVER the years, which is why I wrote my books. I struggled with motivating myself to do it, and struggled getting my oldest child to like it. He's always had a negative attitude towards family night. And since he was my first child, that made it difficult for me to want to keep doing it.

However, the thing that kept me going was discovering there really was a different spirit in our home when we held FHE. It was so noticeable that I couldn't deny where it came from. And it wasn't just during that night—that spirit lasted all week!

I noticed that when we went several weeks or even months without home evening, our home felt different. I was less kind and patient, and there was more fighting. And conversely, when we held it consistently each week, I noticed we all got along better, the children were happier (not perfect, but happier), and I had more patience. Even our marriage had fewer problems.

It's hard though, because Satan really works to prevent home evening. I feel tired and unmotivated, and want to give up, which leads to guilt. When that happens, I have to pray and ask for help to "want" to have it again. So I put my eight-year-old (I love that age, they are so eager to be good) in charge and tell her to get it going again and she does.

One lesson stands out as very special. It was my turn to teach, and to be honest, I had put it off until family night was starting. I had no idea what I was going to do but figured as a professional teacher I could wing it. As we sat down on the couch, I looked over and noticed the picture book *You are Special* by Max Lucado. We had read it before but not for a while. So for the lesson, I read the story. We stopped along the way and discussed what each part of the story was teaching us and about the message of the book—that we are children of God and He loves us for who we are. As we read and talked, the Spirit was stronger than I can ever remember during a family night. By the end, we were all crying. I knew they knew it was true—that God loved them and they were special. It was a simple lesson but so powerful and important for them to learn. I know it's something neither they nor I will ever forget.

The best way I've found to get my children's involvement is to put them in charge. We discuss what responsibilities go on the chart. My eight-year-old is in charge of changing it each week. She also reminds everyone before Monday what his or her responsibility is. By putting my children in charge, I don't worry about keeping their attention because we're doing what they want to do. The children find topics they are interested in and can teach. I have a box of lessons I've collected over the years, and they can choose one from there if they want. They also use the *Friend* magazine or read from a picture book.

We, as parents, also take turns teaching lessons, and I usually don't have a problem with them listening then, either (except for the two-year-old and sometimes the sixteen-year-old).

I've also found that family home evening doesn't have to be long or complicated to reap the blessings; in fact, some of our best lessons have been short and sweet (like my example above). Just by gathering each week, praying, and learning, we receive the blessings.

Anna Jones Buttimore *lives in the South of England and works part time from home for a legal charity. She is the author of three novels,* Haven *and* A World Away *under her former married name, Anna Jones, and* Easterfield.

★ ★ Wait Until Home Evening ★ ★

THE WHOLE FAMILY ARE AT HOME, AND it's Monday evening. The children and I look expectantly at my new husband—the worthy priesthood holder, returned missionary (returned from Russia, no less) and member of the Elders Quorum Presidency—to whom I am sealed for time and all eternity.

"What?" he says. "I don't know how to do family home evening. I've never done it before."

Like me, my husband came from a non-member family and joined the LDS church as an adult, but he then lived alone for several years before I moved into the ward and swept him off his feet, and he had never seen the need to hold family home evening by himself. Spiritual giant though he is, it's not surprising that finding himself overnight the head of a ready-made family, he wasn't immediately able to give a lesson on a gospel theme and hand out relevant music, activity, and refreshment assignments. So we improvised.

After a while we realised that going out for junk food and doing the weekly grocery shop was not really an appropriate family home evening. Happily, we also discovered a great source of inspiration for family night—and I don't mean the Internet. Our ideas come directly from our family.

Whenever one of the children asks, "Why is Primary called Primary?" or "Does popcorn really grow on apricot trees?" we ask them to wait until Monday night for their answer. And when family home evening arrives, their answer might include learning that girls were only invited to join Primary in 1878 because the singing didn't "sound as well as it should," or stringing popcorn onto the apple tree in the garden (apricots don't grow in the British climate).

When our eldest daughter announced that she was becoming vegetarian, we read Doctrine and Covenants 89:10–20 and talked about how we might best honor this counsel and support Gwen in her decision. We decided to eat vegetarian meals as a family twice a week, cut suitable recipes from old magazines, and made a simple vegetarian snack.

The best family home evening we have had to date came about because my daughters, like little girls everywhere, love ponies and riding, and asked that matters equestrian be the theme of our activities and lesson. So we acted out Numbers 22:20–34 with each of them taking turns being the donkey amid much hilarity. And somewhere in there they learned about being obedient to the Lord's commandments.

After two years of marriage, my husband is now a family home evening pro. Like me, he has developed the habit of mentally filing away interests, events, dilemmas, and questions, and turning them into something for family home evening. If anything needs to be planned, discussed, answered, announced, considered, changed, or challenged in our home, it has to wait for Monday night.

Arlen L. Card *graduated from Brigham Young University with degrees in music and in law. He is an accomplished professional performer and studio musician on saxophone and other instruments, and was given a Fellowship to Sundance Institute's Film Composers' Lab. Arlen studied with artists such as Alan Sylvestri, David Newman, Bruce Broughton, and Henry Mancini, receiving numerous composition awards, including those from Telly, Aurora, Barlow, Mayhew, and the Utah Songwriters' Guild.*

★ ★ Family Biz ★ ★

OUR FAMILY AGE RANGE IS FROM COLLEGE to pre-school, and they all know family home evening on Monday night is the time we get together. It is untouchable. On the rare occasion that an older child has to work Monday evening, then we shift to Sunday.

For the sake of the little ones (and the not-so-little ones), we make sure each FHE is as short and memorable as possible. We do this by rotating teachers, and limiting the lesson portion, before the activity, to twenty minutes.

One thing my wife and I learned from friends, and which we adopted for our family, is something we call "Family Biz." After the song, prayer, and lesson, we go around the room (or sometimes go youngest to oldest, or vice versa) and everyone gets a turn to brag about one wonderful thing that happened during the week. This is a much-loved moment, and it's sometimes hard getting them to hold off from telling us eight or nine things.

We've found over the years that if the meeting is fun as well as inspirational, it holds attention a lot better. Not that we cheapen or make light of spiritual things, but a fast pace, and engaging teaching centering on stories keeps everyone interested. We've never had one FHE where someone said, "Oh no! We have to do that again?"

Debbie Coon *is a professional singer and the niece of gifted song artists, Wanda West Palmer and Mildred West Wiseman Packard. Debbie is a profressional singers and the niece of gifted song arts, Wanda West Palmer and Mildred West Wiseman Packard. Debbie's first CD was titled* Come And Never Leave, *and her latest recording is* You Are Loved.

★ ★ All the Right Ingredients ★ ★

M Y HUSBAND, RON, AND I FEEL OUR family has most definitely benefited by coming together every Monday night. This is the time we can be reminded and taught why we are here and how much our Heavenly Father loves us and wants us to come back to live with Him. It has always been a time our children can ask us any question they might have. We have an active family, but even if we've just returned from a week's vacation at Lake Powell, if it's Monday night, Ron makes sure we get a lesson based on the scriptures.

Our son Jonathan, who is serving a mission in Scotland, wrote to us as follows. "Thank you for your uplifting letters . . . Keep studying the scriptures, and having family home evening . . . I have a testimony of doing that, and how it strengthened our family in so many ways. Thank you so much, Dad, for always getting the family together. I love you all. Elder Coon."

One home evening that sticks in my mind is when Ron was a ward missionary. We invited a neighborhood family to bake a cake with us and discussed how each ingredient was important for the cake to turn out right. Not following instructions could make it burn or be too salty. Similarly, Heavenly Father gave us instructions with all the right ingredients to apply to our lives. The Spirit was so strong that evening, leaving a lasting memory with everyone there.

Emily Cushing *compiled the inspirational calendar,* One Heart, Many Voices, *which contains uplifting thoughts from Relief Society sisters around the world. Emily is the creator and moderator of the blog,* Give Away Today.

★ ★ Safety First ★ ★

HOW DOES THE OLD SAYING GO? ITS fun until somebody gets hurt? That is exactly what comes to mind when I think of a combined Singles family home evening I attended one Monday evening while a junior at BYU. My roommates and I gathered with other FHE groups for a barbecue and games in the park. The barbeque consisted of mingling, eating, laughing, and of course, flirting (which seemed to be the objective of many of the FHE activities in my BYU's singles ward). Unfortunately, no one considered the need for safety rules as darkness descended.

Before sunset, the coordinators called everyone over to a grassy field to participate in lawn games. The first game was a unique game of tag. To play this game, you link arms with another participant. When there are enough partners, they form an outer circle; additional people link arms in like manner to form a smaller circle within the bigger circle. The space between the two circles become a track for the person who was "it" to chase others. You stand with arms linked with your partner until someone runs around and links arms on the other side of your partner. At this point, you take off running in between the two circles and hope that you are not touched by the person who was "it."

People were running, and people were laughing. All were having a great time. Then my roommate (linked to someone close to me on the outer circle) and I noticed that due to limited visibility, people running around the inner circle could not tell when someone else was running towards them in the opposite direction. It seemed as though a head-on collision was bound to happen. My roommate commented that the game had become a little dangerous.

That's when the inevitable happened. A tall redheaded guy was running at top speed around the inner circle in our direction. At that exact moment, a small dark-haired girl came around the circle from the opposite direction. Right in front of my roommate and me, the two collided with incredible force. We heard a huge "POP" as they smacked faces and were thrown backwards off their feet.

The circles quickly dispersed as everyone ran to aid the injured. The redheaded guy and the dark-haired girl were both lying on the ground covering their faces. The point of impact had been her forehead and his teeth. As a result, it looked as though his two front teeth were missing. However, they were pushed completely backwards against the roof of his mouth. An ugly bump with a deep gash had formed on the girl's forehead.

The activity for the guy and the girl ended in disaster. Unless, of course, they flirted on the way to the hospital. And if that's the case, then the night was not a total loss after all.

We learned a valuable lesson in putting safety first.

Marco Davis *and daughters,* **Rebecca, Kathryn,** *and* **Elizabeth** *formed a folk group known as Fiddle-Sticks, which performs music from the Celtic lands, England, and America. They have eight award-winning albums (most recent—*Farewell to Nauvoo *and* Ampersand*); have numerous Pearl Award nominations; and won the Best Contemporary Instrumental Recording Award from the Faith Centered Music Association. They have performed nationwide, appeared on television and radio, and were official 2002 Salt Lake Olympics Cultural Arts performers.*

Home Evening Talent Keeps ★ ★ on Growing ★ ★

W E HAD MANY MUSICAL FAMILY HOME EVENINGS. Essentially, when the kids were young, family night was a quick prayer and song and maybe a lesson, but mostly it was about the "Talent" part—each sister showed off what she had learned in music lessons. Many of these activities evolved into impromptu jam sessions. As the kids grew up, the jam sessions (or even intentional arranging of tunes to perform) became a bigger part of our home evenings. On a few occasions, we invited other families who played music to come over. We shared tunes and played together. As long as the evening included pizza or ice cream, it was a guaranteed success!

We sometimes performed on Mondays and found that many other families enjoyed watching the occasional show for a home evening special. When living on the east coast, the girls performed with their mom at Renaissance fairs, parties, and the Washington DC Temple Visitor Center—and of course, in church. After moving to Utah, we helped sponsor a Provo Arts Center music series on Monday nights that for a couple of years had a loyal following of families. Other libraries or civic groups invited us to perform—always billed as family friendly concerts.

We've also toured the United States, Europe, and Japan with our music—a blend of traditional Celtic styles, with jazz, folk, rock, and even bluegrass mixed in. Many concerts (especially when the girls were young teens) generated conversations with other parents about how to "get your kids to practice" or "how to start a family band." We always had to admit we never started out planning to have a family band, but just began playing together for fun in family home evenings and let it evolve from there. Like Becca says, "The band has been a positive thing for our family. We have the most wonderful times together because it's such a creative process."

My first wife, and mother of the girls, was Kira Pratt Davis. She was an accomplished Irish folk harpist and singer. When Kira died of cancer in 1997, the girls had an extra incentive to play music together. It was a way for them to remember their mother and carry on her music. They took over the job of writing and arranging music for the group, and I joined them on stage on the Irish drum (called the "bodhran") and guitar. Playing music together helped get us through those tough years. On stage, we had to put on a happy face, even when it was hard. It was a kind of musical family therapy.

While each of the band members has developed her own style over the years, they all recognize their mother as the ultimate source. Becca explains, "Much of what we know about performing, arranging music, and putting on a show together is my mom's signature style."

All three sisters are now married and living from coast to coast. But the music of FiddleSticks plays on. Like Liz says, "It seems we can't find ourselves in the same city without putting on a reunion concert or two." Their mom would understand and would be proud of the musical journey she started during family home evenings many years ago.

Jeffrey J. Denning, *CPS, CMAS, is an Iraq War Veteran, a counterterrorism specialist, and former Federal Air Marshal. He writes an Aviation Security blog for the* Washington Times *and has been featured on CNN, Anderson Cooper 360, Fox News, CBS, documentary films, and radio stations around the world.*

★ ★ Iraq Home Evening ★ ★

MY MOM HAD SIX CHILDREN AND, UNFORTUNATELY, a pretty rough divorce. Even to this day, I distinctly remember coming home one Sunday afternoon from Primary overwhelmed by powerful feelings of joy, comfort, and peace. This incredible feeling of the spirit coursed through my heart and mind because of a new song we learned that day in Primary: "Families Can Be Together Forever." But my parents are divorced and I have a broken family that won't be together, I remember thinking. Yet, I had hope for the future—my future family.

Despite the challenges of raising six children mostly on her own, my mom had the drive to keep the Lord's commandments and the courage to hold family home evening. It was a struggle, no doubt. As rowdy children, we didn't make it easy for her. In fact, we missed holding regular family home evening sometimes for several weeks for one reason or another, but our mother was determined. She must have wanted to give up at times, but she didn't. I recall her energy to recharge and restart repeatedly. Her determination to obey served as a more powerful example and lesson to me and my siblings than the less-than-perfect home evening gatherings.

Many years later, after starting a family of my own, I incorporated those same powerful lessons that influenced my childhood. My wife and I began the tradition of singing "Families Can Be Together Forever" with our children right from the start.

While working shift work as a police officer, living in Jerusalem and working as a U.S. government contractor, traveling out of
town as an undercover Federal Air Marshal, or serving in Iraq with
the U.S. Army Reserves, my wife was the glue that held our family
together. Whenever I was home, we held regular family home evening. Although my wife was often alone and facing many pressures
and burdens of her own, she was committed to holding home evening
whenever I was gone. While in Iraq, she sent me a video recording of
several things from home—among them was a family night, with our
rowdy children who didn't seem to be paying attention at all.

During one of the most stressful, trying, and difficult times of my
life, towards the end of my year-long military deployment to Iraq, I
was able to call home one day. My sweet companion was anxious to
share some exciting news with me and she put our youngest daughter
at the time (then just two years old) on the phone. Before I left for Iraq,
our baby girl couldn't even say "Daddy," but on the phone she sang to
me the entire song of "Families Can Be Together Forever." My heart
melted. Welling tears of gratitude for my wife and love for each of our
children accompanied my effervescent smile.

Today, it fills my heart with great joy and gratitude to gather as a
family every Monday night. I'm forever grateful that my wife taught
our children when I couldn't be around to help her. Most importantly,
I've learned that while no family is perfect and no family home evening goes quite the way we'd like them to, if we try our hardest to do
what's right, the Lord will make up where we lack.

Tullio DeRuvo *was the first Italian to serve a mission in Utah, 1984–86. He owns Il Grande Noce, the only LDS publishing company in Italy, and has written several young adult books, including* A Tree Named Joshua. *Tullio lectures in seminars around the country, and is Italy's National Director of Public Affairs for the Church.*

★ ★ Is It That Bad? ★ ★

I WAS REARED IN A TYPICAL ITALIAN family; we were Catholics, but my good mother was uneasy about it. She had unanswered questions and was praying to find the truth when the missionaries knocked on our door. After baptism, we started holding family home evenings. It was awkward, something we weren't used to. As teenagers, we had a hard time sharing spiritual thoughts and feelings. We gave Mother much frustration. When on my mission, I resolved to get my own kids used to FHE early. It would be nice and sweet every Monday night.

Some twenty years later, I found myself living déjà-vu. Why did my son have basketball practice on Monday nights? Why was I ready to hold FHE when my wife was not, and vice versa? Why did my lovely twin girls quarrel right before starting? Our lack of consistency made things forced and unnatural. Sometimes we had wonderful experiences. But only sometimes.

Because of lack of planning, the results were unpredictable, but we were going to do something about it—some day. Meanwhile, our FHE's were casual, good time spent together.

The call to repentance came when Elder Richard G. Scott from the Quorum of Twelve Apostles visited our stake. We had a special meeting with over a thousand people attending. I was his interpreter. I became uneasy when in the middle of his talk he called Giulia and Viola, my twin girls, onto the stand and asked them questions about family life. He asked, "How does your dad help your mom when she's in need?" Viola answered, "He calls us and tells us to go and help." The audience roared. So he asked, "I mean, what does HE do to help?" Silence and panic in their eyes. Elder Scott said, "Is it THAT bad?" Finally, Giulia added, "Well, he cooks. Sometimes." Elder Scott changed subject. "Do you hold family home evenings?" Silence. Then Viola said, "Well, we used to, but that was long ago." That brought another roar. I stood next to the three of them, translating, and sweating. "Do you have family prayers?" Silence. "Don't you pray at meals, at least?" Giulia: "Oh yes, we do."

Imagine my face color. Nailed by my own daughters in front of thousands.

After the meeting, I asked them why they answered that way. They said they were in such panic they couldn't think straight. I took responsibility for not holding regular home evenings—but the rest! It all sounded so awful! The good news is shocking experiences help us change. When next Monday night came, friends from all wards in our stake called to tease and remind me to hold family home evening. I told them I would never miss one again for the rest of my life.

And I didn't. All it took was the right mindset. We made time to prepare instead of improvising, and gave heed to President Hinckley's suggestion to keep lessons short and sweet. Then we enjoyed ourselves. Family members looked forward to it. We had a few grunts here and there, but our Monday nights changed, and the rest of our weeks with them.

Elder Scott was great. During his talk, he gave powerful testimony; there were no dry eyes. That experience changed many people's lives. It certainly changed ours. If you too need a little jumpstart, always keep in mind: Elder Scott may come to *your* stake next time.

Eric Dodge *is a Country music singer who performs throughout the U.S. and Canada. In 2004, Eric was named Southern Utah's winner of the Colgate Country Showdown. His radio single, "Anything for You," hit #19 on the New Music Weekly-Independent Artists chart. Eric has shared the stage with many of Nashville's finest country music stars including the late Chris Ledoux, Diamond Rio, Little Texas, Collin Raye, and SHeDAISY.*

★ ★ Nothing as Valuable as Family ★ ★

WHEN I WAS A KID, MY FAMILY always had home evening. We did everything from lessons to just spending time as family. I remember many of those lessons, especially around Christmas. We got together for FHE and talked about the true meaning of Christmas, the star, the wise men, and Jesus. Then we talked about Santa Claus, of course, and Mom helped our family create a fun thirty-day chart on which we glued butterscotch and starlight mints for each day up to the twenty-fifth.

I remember countless family nights when the whole family watched a movie or played games, and I know these were some of the best moments of my life. As my siblings and I grew older and more rebellious, we fought against having home evening, and wanted to spend time with friends. It wasn't cool to be with family anymore. Looking back, I wish more than anything we'd continued attending those family nights. Friends are important, but there's nothing as valuable as family.

As we grew into young adults, our parents never gave up trying, often gathering us all for family night dinner. I know our parents' persistence with home evening is why we are all close today. My family is involved in my country music career and travel around the country with me whenever possible. I look forward to the day when I have a family of my own. There is no doubt in my mind that we will hold family home evening.

Brian Fairrington *has created award-winning editorial cartoons nationally syndicated to over 800 newspapers and publications in America with Cagle Cartoons. His cartoons have appeared in the* New York Times, USA Today, *and on* CNN, MSNBC *and* Fox News. *Additionally, his cartoons regularly appear on MSNBC's popular Cagle Cartoon Index. Brian also authored the* Best Political Cartoons of the Year *books.*

★ ★ Secret Santa Service ★ ★

Spending quality family time together is one of the most important things we can do as parents.

I recall being bored sometimes during childhood home evenings, but now that I'm older, with a family of my own, I look back on those earlier times with great fondness.

Around the holidays one year, my wife and I gave a lesson on service in our home evening. Our children had questions about what service to others really meant. So my wife and I decided to have our family play "Secret Santa" to a non-member family that lived down the street from us.

The father had been left with three small children. I knew through a mutual acquaintance that the man worked overtime to make extra money for Christmas presents. We decided this was a perfect opportunity for our children to learn about helping others.

We took the children shopping for gifts. Our children were similar in age to theirs, and it was natural to want the toys for themselves. This initially proved to be difficult for my wife and me as we gently tried to explain that these toys we not for them but for another family who needed them more. After a few moments, our daughter, who was four at the time, said the dolly she had picked out would be perfect for the other little girl. Our boys followed, saying the other boys would appreciate the Spiderman car and video game just as much as they would.

We wrapped the gifts on the back tailgate of our suburban in the parking lot. Then we placed all the gifts in a large brown box and headed quickly to the other family's house. We turned off the lights, parked, and walked up the long cold street. Our children became excited at the notion of leaving presents for someone to find the next morning and we had to quiet them down or blow our cover.

I laid the box down at the doorstep, and we all hustled down the street into the warm cabin of our SUV.

All the way home, our children were jumping with excitement at what we had accomplished. My wife and I took the opportunity to explain to them that the warm feelings they had were far greater than any brief moments of pleasure they would have received if the toys we bought that night would have gone home with us.

They still talk about that night several years later.

Rob Ficiur *from Canada, is the author of the* Time Traveller in Church History *series, which so far includes* Rescue the Prophet *and* Trouble in Palmyra.

★ ★ Pageant Opens Teen Mouths ★ ★

GROWING UP IN A PART-MEMBER FAMILY, I envied all the stories I heard about the blessings of family home evening. When my wife (a convert) and I married, we held home evening weekly.

As we raised six children, home evening often seemed like it was designed to test the patience of the parents who tried to organize it. One Monday, home evening turned into Family Fight Night. We sent all the children to bed without a snack and without home evening. Three days later, one of my sons (approximately five years old) asked a question I will never forget. "We missed family home evening on Monday. When are we going to have it this week?"

What was he missing? The lessons, no matter how well planned, never seemed to be like those magnificent spiritual experiences I had heard and read about. But even though the children wiggled and argued, they learned something. They knew that each week we set aside one night to be with our family and were obeying modern prophets' advice to "do it."

In 2001 our family was blessed to be part of the Hill Cumorah Pageant cast. When we got the acceptance letter, we used FHE to make the announcement. I held a toy airplane and pretended to fly somewhere. But where? When the boys, ages ranging from four to sixteen, figured out where we going, they were ecstatic. Being in the 2001 Pageant Cast was the experience of a lifetime.

In 2004 our second oldest son (age seventeen) was accepted as part of the work crew for the pageant. He flew in a week early and came back a week later. He told us that he had a great experience. But had we not asked him to do a FHE lesson on the subject, we would only have seen the tip of the ice berg of what he had learned. As our son gave this home evening lesson, I was astounded. Who was this speaking? Was this a twenty-one-year-old returned missionary? No, he was a seventeen-year-old entering his senior year of high school. He spoke about the "tender mercies of the Lord" that allowed him to partake of the blessings of the pageant and of the gospel. I don't remember any other words he said, but I remember the power with which he spoke them. The same spirit that he had found at Hill Cumorah was there with us. Having him teach us allowed our son to share spiritual insights beyond his years.

Three years later another son returned from a week at Especially for Youth. We knew he had a great time because he wouldn't take his bracelet off. When we questioned him further about his experiences, we got a few sentences of information. When we asked him to do a home evening lesson on things he learned from EFY, the power and insight gained by a quiet teenager came forth through the spirit in a powerful way.

One summer we decided to have some Hot Dog Home Evenings. My wife sent invitations around to non-member neighbors, and we had hot dog roasts. The first week only one couple came over, and we visited in ways we had never done before. We never knew who would come—but it was fine whether we had two people or twenty. Inviting friends to some of our home evenings helped our family enjoy more opportunities for missionary work.

Sergio Flores *is Spain's National Director of Public Affairs. He has received awards from the Business School of Lleida University, and AECOOP-ARAGON, The Association for Co-operative Studies, for outstanding contributions in the field of Management Skills. He is the author and co-author of ten books including* 50 Values for Success *and* Values to be Better.

★ ★ Sweetest Memories ★ ★

FAMILY HOME EVENING HAS BEEN ONE OF the greatest blessings of my life for me and my family. We learned truths of the restored gospel and gained more union and communication, which led to an increase of love among family members. Home evening is the right occasion for learning teachings of the living prophets, to have fun, and to cultivate a good sense of humour.

I remember one family night when our youngest child, Sergio, was eight years old. I was explaining the Second Coming: "Look, He is coming with the clouds, and every eye will see Him" (Rev. 1:7) Sergio rapidly raised his arm and asked: "What about the blind ones?" The way he said it was funny and we laughed in amazement at his insight, then explained how the blind, too, would see or understand in their own way.

All family members have learned many good things: to conduct music, play the piano, and share talents and the gospel with others. Home evenings helped the family make worthy decisions, such as attending seminary and institute, serving missions, and getting married and sealed in the Lord's House. I can gladly say, "The sweetest moments of my life have been those I spent with my family, my beloved eternal treasury, at home, in family home evening."

Jessie Clark Funk *shares her music with people from across the United States, Europe, and Africa. She has released three CD's called* Clay in His Hands, Better than I, *and* Everything Speaks His Name. *In 2001, she toured the U.S. with the Broadway musical* Footloose. *Jessie sang the national anthem for the Utah Jazz, performed for Vice President Dick Cheney, and won the 2004 Best of State award for Best Female Vocalist. She is also an eight-time FCMA Pearl Award winner.*

★ ★ Keeping It Simple ★ ★

MY FAVORITE FAMILY HOME EVENING MEMORY WAS when my husband and I took our three-year-old daughter outside for an evening walk and asked her to find different items in nature. She found a leaf, a rock, a flower, and then pointed to the sky. We asked her where all these great natural wonders came from, and together we all learned that rocks, flowers, and the sky all came from our Heavenly Father who loves us.

This was an easy activity that only took about ten minutes. But it was effective and fun for us. We added some singing time with a few primary songs and then went out for ice cream cones.

I wish someone had told me when I first became a mother that it was okay to have simple home evenings like this one. When my daughter was just a baby, I became discouraged because there weren't very many options for activities we could do with such a little child. So, if I could offer any advice to young couples with small children, it would be to not worry about having long, deep lessons. Keeping it simple benefits everyone.

Lynn Gardner, *best selling author of* Vanished: A Maggi McKenzie Mystery *and its sequal,* Pursued, *is also author of the "jewel" mystery series:* Topaz and Treachery, Diamonds and Danger, Pearls and Peril, *and many more.*

★ ★ Family Circus ★ ★

F OR NEARLY TWENTY-FIVE YEARS, WE WERE A typical Air Force family with a frequently absent father. Raising four children through the challenges of frequent moves, new friends, new wards or branches, we clung to the apostolic promise that if we regularly held family home evenings, our children would gain testimonies of the gospel and stay faithful in the Church.

But our family home evenings didn't seem like anyone else's. They more closely resembled a family circus with energetic little bodies performing somersaults, cartwheels, acrobatics, and antics that had little resemblance to any teaching situation. An onlooker would have thought a bunch of monkeys had been loosed in the family room, hanging off everything but the chandelier.

We tried to make the lessons short and sweet, stressing just one gospel principle. We tried having them take turns teaching with occasional disastrous results, often hilarious lessons, and sometimes a measure of success. We let them conduct, prepare refreshments, lead the singing, and choose the topics for lessons. I'm sure there wasn't anything that we didn't try at least once, but we truly felt we were failing as parents in the family home evening department.

When my husband was sent to Turkey for fifteen months on an isolated tour, we taped our family home evenings and mailed him the frequently funny results, hoping it would alleviate the loneliness he experienced by missing his family. Sometimes I secretly thought he might be glad he was in Turkey and not home trying to hold some kind of normal family home evening—and failing.

But eventually I was astonished to discover that learning had been taking place. Through all the acrobatics, they were actually listening to the lesson. In spite of the circus atmosphere, they heard what was being taught—and more surprisingly—it stuck.

Once a month, we had an activity that one of the children chose: a safari in the backyard, a trip for ice cream, getting together with another family for fun and treats. The variety of activities and the absence of a formal "sit-down" learning atmosphere became a very positive addition to our agenda.

I wish I could say that I felt our family home evenings were wonderful and that we had been a great example for other members. Unfortunately, I can't. What I can do is testify that it works! I have a very strong testimony that the mechanics may be different for everyone, but as long as you are humbly and diligently teaching the gospel—that counts! Your success will come if for no other reason than you are persevering in faithfully keeping the commandments and obeying the Prophets to teach your children in this way.

Two of our children served missions; all four of our living children were married in the temple. That, for me, spells success. I believe it came about in part because of our obedience in holding family home evening and "enduring to the end" through the laughter and tears of our very strange family home evening circuses.

Stan M. Gardner, *M.D., was trained in traditional Western medicine and is a certified nutrition specialist (CNS). He writes and lectures extensively on the subject of preventive medicine and natural means of healing. His website is at www.stangardnermd.com*

★ ★ Dollar Dinner Night ★ ★

WE HAVE EIGHT CHILDREN, AND IN ADDITION to holding family home evening, we held family home morning. We made it a priority to study the scriptures daily. This often meant gently waking children up when it was their turn to read their two verses, but we were delighted to have the family there, no matter how sleepy they were! We celebrated each time we completed the Book of Mormon, and always asked the children to choose the reward.

As for family home evening, our favorite experiences included "Dollar Dinner Night," when we gave every family member a dollar, and each scurried off into a different part of the store to locate the best food deal for a dollar. At first, we didn't make any particular assignments. We just ate the purchased items. But we soon discovered this did not make for a balanced meal by any stretch of the imagination! So we assigned different children to buy the protein, the veggies, the fruits, bread, and dessert. Sometimes we teamed people up, but not often. It was more fun seeing what everyone bought. Nowadays I recommend increasing the amount. This fun exercise gave us opportunities to discuss nutrition, comparative food values, taste, and ways to save money on our family budget. We also learned what a blessing it is to grow our own food.

Our home evening trips took on significance for us because we kept hymn books in the car, and spent many pleasant hours harmonizing and singing hymns. The children still enjoy singing together, and all of our children have made music an important part of their lives.

H. Wallace Goddard, *Ph.D., CFLE, is a professor and family life specialist for the University of Arkansas Cooperative Extension Service. Among his accomplishments is the creation of a PBS Television series,* Guiding Children Successfully, *revision of the classic parenting book,* Between Parent and Child, *as well as the development of many family resources such as* The Personal Journey, The Parenting Journey. *In addition to his scholarly work, he writes LDS books and a monthly column for MeridianMagazine.com. His most recent books are* Soft-Spoken Parenting *and* Drawing Heaven into Your Marriage.

Building a Bridge from Home Evening to God

IN OUR FAMILY, WE HAVE USED FAMILY home evening for two purposes: to build family closeness, and to teach the gospel of Jesus Christ. To advance the first purpose we have often had fun activities. To advance the second, we have often had lessons. Of course, we try to make the lessons fun, loving, and engaging so that they satisfy both purposes.

Some years ago we found a way to use the teachings in FHE to enlarge family members' love for Heavenly Father and each other. Here's how it happened. One Sunday after a stake conference, as we sat at the dinner table, fifteen-year-old Emily asked a painful question, "Today, in stake conference, when we stood to sing 'I Know that My Redeemer Lives,' I felt so happy . . ." Emily paused, seeming troubled, ". . . that I cried. What does that mean?" Emily seemed to think there was something wrong with her.

Nancy and I rejoiced that Emily had heard the sacred voice of the Spirit! We told her, "Emily, that is the Spirit of God speaking to your soul. The Spirit brings us comfort, teaches us new things, and sometimes we feel so overwhelmed that we cry. We call that feeling joy." We encouraged Emily to notice and cherish any experiences like the one she had in conference.

Because of Emily's experience, we developed a family tradition. Every Sunday at dinner, we ask each family member (and any guests)

if they would share their best experience of the day. The experience might be spiritual or not. Usually it was. Each of us told how we were touched by a musical number, the words of the sacrament prayer, or seeing a beloved friend. We wanted our children to notice and celebrate the feelings that make life joyous. We wanted them to acknowledge the source. And we all wanted to learn from each other's experiences.

We have been indescribably blessed by our sharing of best experiences. Often Emily told us about something in church that touched her heart. Andy might tell about something sweet and powerful that he learned from a beloved Aaronic Priesthood leader. Sara might tell us about a loving encounter with a child whom she baby-sat. My wife often told of her love for fellow Saints. Sometimes I told of spiritual discoveries delivered by the Spirit.

I don't think that family home evening fills the measure of its creation when it is isolated from gospel living. Joining FHE with the sharing of spiritual experiences brings gospel teachings to life and builds our relationships with each other and God. The sharing of best experiences builds a bridge between learning and living.

Even though our children are grown and living in distant cities, they still call us on Sunday afternoons to continue the tradition of sharing their best experiences of the day. We continue to rejoice in God's goodness. We are trying to follow President Eyring's counsel to look for God's hand in our lives.[1]

NOTE

1. Henry B. Eyring, "O Remember, Remember," *Ensign*, Nov. 2007.

Lyle Hadlock *is a master pianist and composer. His music is on BYU Radio and KZION, and he often spends his lunch hour playing at rest homes. Lyle has produced many CD's, including* Songs for the Sabbath *and* We Ever Pray for Thee.

★ ★ Dark and Light ★ ★

WE'VE BEEN CONSISTENT ABOUT HOLDING FAMILY HOME evenings and enjoy spending time together. Even as teenagers, our kids still have a willing attitude. For about ten years, we've used a chart containing responsibilities—one for each family member. This gives our children opportunities to prepare and give lessons, many of which have been creative and interesting. Others have been thoughtful and spiritually touching. It gives family members confidence in their own teaching abilities and many chances to share testimony.

Activities include playing our famous "hide and seek in the dark." We make the house as dark as we can inside—closing all blinds and curtains. Once hidden, no one can change places. The unfinished basement area is off limits as we get too freaked out down there.

It's amazing how simple hiding places become difficult to find when there's no light. We make thorough use of hands, arms, and feet to cover all areas of a room and listen intently. Although this is a fun activity, it can also be a teaching moment for the family when we stop to process it with them afterwards. As with life, we can see and discover things more easily when there is light involved. When we have the light of Christ and a gospel perspective, we more clearly see things as they really are. We have the power of discernment and can more honestly see others and ourselves as God sees us.

Barry Hansen *is a singer-songwriter, free-lance graphic designer, and inspirational speaker. He studied voice and graphic design at BYU and sang with BYU's Vocal Jazz Ensemble. Barry performs frequently and has recorded lead vocals on over a dozen albums, including a solo album,* My Soul Hungered. *He co-writes with his brother and producer, Greg Hansen; some of their newer songs are available online as singles. Barry was a 2004 Pearl Award nominee for Studio Vocalist, a 2006 nominee for Male Vocalist of the Year, and a five-time nominee for Album Design, winning the award in 2004.*

★ ★ Worth It. Despite the Challenges ★ ★

MY WIFE, MARIAN, AND I HAVE A very busy home because we had eight children in a little over ten years (four boys and four girls). We both came from families that consistently held family home evening, so continuing that tradition was a given. Setting aside Monday night for family home evening was always a priority, which sometimes meant saying no to other Monday night activities. Besides Monday night, my wife has always been careful to avoid activities and commitments that would take us away from home too much on other days as well. One of our teenagers referred to this once when she half-jokingly said something like, "We're always together! We don't need family home evening, we need 'family apart night!' "

It has been a challenge to keep everyone involved and paying attention, especially when the children were little. Out of necessity, we try to keep FHE simple. Sometimes, we write to missionaries serving from our ward or extended family. We hand out a piece of paper to each child, and he or she writes or draws (or both) a message to the missionary. We see quite a bit of creativity with this activity, and sometimes the missionaries send back a thank-you letter.

Another traditional home evening at our house, especially around Christmas time, is getting out the hymn books and singing together. Instead of just an opening and closing song, we spend the entire time singing. Some of the children like this better than others.

We usually have a brief lesson. Some memorable ones have been

presented by our sons, who were working on Duty to God requirements. They have put on sock puppet plays about the Ten Lepers and
the Good Samaritan, and even produced a live-action movie with puppets called *Daniel and the Lion's Den*.

One recent successful lesson was about my father and mother. Both
died relatively young, so our children only knew one set of grand-
parents. I shared short bios of my parents and told stories about them,
more than I had planned to because the children were so interested in
learning about them.

But most of the time, "quick and easy" is what's needed, so the
children or we will use a single picture from the Gospel Art Picture
Kit, or a single paragraph from The Strength of Youth pamphlet as the
basis for the lesson.

Sometimes we have an activity after the lesson, such as trips to the
library or playing Hide and Seek, although the latter can be challenging for me because I'm six feet four, and it's hard to find a place to hide
a big body. When the weather's nice, we have picnics in the canyon or
pizza in the park.

Some of our FHEs haven't turned out very well because of lack
of preparation or grouchy moods. But in spite of the challenges, we
feel family night is worth doing because it adds stability to home life,
provides teaching moments, helps develop talents, and increases family
unity.

Jennie Hansen *is the Whitney Award-winning author of twelve novels, including The Bracelet series, and whose latest book is titled High Country. Other publications include newspaper and magazines articles, and LDS book reviews. She is a frequent speaker at firesides and conferences.*

★ ★ Forgotten? ★ ★

THEY'VE FORGOTTEN. I'M SERIOUS—MY CHILDREN DON'T REMEMBER having family home evenings when they were small.

"Don't you remember the times we had a short lesson then went to Bishop Kelsey's ice cream parlor?"

"That was a neat place. I remember Janice wouldn't eat ice cream unless she got a cone decorated like a clown."

"What about the month all of our lessons were on genealogy and we went to the library to see how many of our ancestors we could find in history books or encyclopedias?"

"I found Henry Wadsworth Longfellow," our oldest daughter recalled. "Isn't he a sixteenth cousin or something?"

"And there were all those kings and knights," our son added.

"I remember Eleanor of Aquitaine," another daughter volunteered. "Wasn't she married to both the king of France and later to the king of England?"

"I remember that too. She had a son who was Dad's ancestor, and he already had an illegitimate son who was Mom's ancestor. So way back—we never did figure out how many generations back—Mom and Dad are cousins."

"I looked up a famous pirate that night and tried to find out about two great-great-uncles you said both served jail time for making moonshine," my son contributed to the conversation again.

"I thought you didn't remember having family home evenings?"

I reminded our children, who are all adults now and were discussing family home evenings following a family dinner.

"I remember doing those things, but I didn't know they were family home evenings," our third daughter said. I felt like a failure, hurt and disappointed, as I thought back to the special dinners, some served by candlelight, the lessons I'd prepared, the games and crafts we'd used to enliven lessons, and our attempts to include the children in the planning, preparing musical numbers, and saying simple prayers. She continued, "I kind of remember sitting around taking turns reading scriptures. Janice drove me nuts, she read so slow."

"She was six years younger than you," I protested. "She was in the first grade when you started junior high."

"It was good practice in being patient for my mission. I met some people there who were adults and as slow as she was. I told myself that I survived listening to her, so there was hope."

As I examined their comments and considered the loving parents they've become, I concluded they must have absorbed something. They grew up with a deep love for each other and testimonies of the gospel, and those with children are holding regular family home evenings.

Michael Hansen *and his wife,* **Signhild,** *from Sweden, own Svenska LantChips. Signhild Hansen is renowned in Sweden as vice president of Business Europe, the organization for twenty-two million private European enterprises. Signhild won the Ruter Dam of the Year Award, and is Board Chairman of the Confederation of Swedish Enterprise, and a board member of the King Carl XVI Foundation for Young Leadership.*

Home Evening Turns Handicap ★ ★ Into Blessings ★ ★

OUR FIRST CHILD, RICHARD, WAS BORN PREMATURELY in 1987. Lack of oxygen during the birth process gave him handicaps for life. Since then, we have been blessed with another five children. The first ten years after Richard's birth, our time was filled with doctor's appointments and trying to figure out the best ways to help Richard.

Richard never had the peace of mind to participate in our home evenings as the other children have done. His restlessness and inability to read and write put a lot of obstacles before him and prevented him from enjoying the triumphs of mastering chores like coloring within borders of a frame, reading a word without heavy strain, threading a needle, and so on. Failure was always around the corner and always discouraging for him. After many fruitless attempts, Richard was allowed to wander off after the opening prayer and come back for refreshments. The other five children were given a different pace in the learning process. For years, I took Richard apart, both for FHE and also for Sunday School and other Church activities in order to open opportunities for a father and a son to be together and discuss important things in life.

Despite Richard's bad start in life, what could have been a string of failures and helplessness has been transformed into a string of successes, not only for Richard, but for all of us. The difference between the two is found in principles we learn from the gospel. As parents, we are stewards and are expected to use our intelligence, resources, and gifts to bless each other in situations like family home evening. We are each other's keeper.

By adapting personalized approaches and highlighting progress, pushing for Richard to develop his points of keen interest, we believe that we have been on our way to success since our first home evening. Determination to carry through leads to success. As Richard reaches adulthood in a state of harmony, embracing life, we look back and wonder how all this could happen, despite the odds. Giving talks in Primary and in sacrament meetings in spite of a serious speech handicap; becoming an honorary member of a voluntary fire department; becoming our own full-fledged fire-prevention specialist; riding his bike farther and farther away from his neighborhood; and relying on his family are proofs that his life is a success. The steadfast course pointed out for us through the power of the gospel joined together with the prospect of eternal life are the fuel that helps this happen.

It is wonderful to see the fruits of Gospel principles. As parents, we proactively develop skills to meet and master challenges together with our children. We show them that they are not alone. The gospel and the weekly routines we carry out as members of the Savior's Church makes us very special—and very responsible for each other.

On September 19, 2008, Richard and his brother, David, were set apart as missionaries. David was called to serve in Birmingham, England. Richard was set apart as a full-time service missionary—an assistant gardener and janitor in the Stockholm Temple. For Richard to serve a mission is more than we ever expected or hoped for. A true blessing for him and his entire family.

Dr. David Glen Hatch *is an international concert and recording artist and distinguished teacher of piano, who enjoys an active career as a soloist and guest artist with numerous chamber and symphony orchestras on five continents. In 2004, Dr. Hatch was the American pianist invited to perform with the Ukraine National Symphony in Kiev to commemorate the 100-year anniversary of the birth of world-renowned Russian pianist, Vladimir Horowitz. Two of his CDs have received Grammy Award nominations for Best Classical and Patriotic Albums, and Best Instrumental Soloist with Orchestra.*

 Getting to Know Them

WHEN OUR FAMILY WAS YOUNGER WITH ALL our children at home, we invited a different family from our ward once each month to share family home evening with us. They were assigned to provide the lesson and we provided the refreshments.

We found this an enjoyable way of getting to know our ward family while making new friends. Many excellent and varied topics, experiences, and activities from other backgrounds were shared with our family, and our children enjoyed learning more about each other. The invited family would bring prepared questionnaires for each participant to fill out. Questions varied from "What is your favorite color, food, or dessert?" to "Share your most embarrassing moment." Answers were read to the group with everyone guessing the person who wrote them.

Guy Hedderwick *has been CEO of three major sports clubs in South Africa: Border Rugby, Hellenic Football, and Black Leopards, another professional soccer team (third largest in the country). He then went to New Zealand and became CEO of New Zealand's only professional soccer team, the New Zealand Knights Football Club.*

Home Evening in
★ ★ Many Places ★ ★

I WAS A BEGRUDGING FATHER—ALWAYS INTERESTED IN playing sport or working in it professionally. It was my life until I had children. Now, I feel so humble to be blessed with four wonderful, beautiful, and different children. Business and sport is often about making good, quick decisions and the best one I ever made was asking Mandy to marry me fairly soon after meeting her. I'm a convert to the gospel (Mandy insisted I hear the missionaries) and Mandy is a fourth generation member. Mandy's great-grandfather was a founding member in our home country of South Africa. This makes our four children fifth generation and gives us a huge responsibility to ensure this wonderful heritage continues.

We led busy lives, having forged my career traveling all over the world from Europe to Asia, Africa, and currently New Zealand, where we've already lived in three cities. Working in a professional sports environment can be exciting, but potentially disruptive. However, because family is so important to us and we wanted our children to grow up as good, solid members of the church, holding family home evening has kept us grounded and has been an opportunity to bond. I've learned the importance of prayer in our family, which has molded our children. I believe family night has a similar advantage.

Our activities divide into a number of categories, from learning, to cultural and family favorites, which include physical activities. One favorite is nature walking. We take the dogs into the countryside or forests near our home. Mandy tells the children stories about how certain things are formed and lessons about our bodies; why heart rates are elevated; why we get hot; and the difference between a fruit fly and us. These activities work best for us because of the age range—fifteen, eight, six, and five.

We recently walked around the inland lagoon and up into the forest and learned about gravity, erosion, and the human body. Even I listened closely as Mandy explained these wonders of nature to the children. Sometimes, I think I learn more than the kids from these lessons. It is absolutely incredible how little we know and how much we still need to learn if we want to be like our Heavenly Father one day. On our way home, we discussed the importance of following instructions and staying away from the edge of the cliff. We learned how Heavenly Father wants us to also stay as far away from the edge as possible and not flirt with sin and trouble. A valuable lesson for our fifteen-year-old.

The hardest activity for us is working together on a service project. The two young boys find it difficult to stay on task, which annoys the older girl and boy. Doing things together as a family can sometimes be tough, but I know families who try are tighter knit and less likely to go inactive. Children who learn from parents generally do well at school and forge successful careers—and more importantly, successful families. It's tempting at times to give up and let everyone watch television when we're tired, (or children seem uninterested), and it's all too much effort—until I hear our children repeat back to my wife and me some pearl of wisdom we imparted to them. I think we do them, and ourselves, a disservice if we fail to engage them in family home evening.

Sarah Hinze *is an author and speaker who has appeared on national radio and television, and lectured at colleges and universities around the U.S. Sarah's many books include* The Castaways, We Lived in Heaven, *and* Songs of the Morning Stars. *Currently, Sarah is working with the Village Connection as an Education Consultant. She develops educational seminars for families. In 1992 she was named Arizona Homemaker of the Year.*

★ ★ Celebrating the One ★ ★

WE HAVE BEEN BLESSED WITH NINE CHILDREN, born within a period of nineteen years. We are true experts in fatigue, frustration, chaos, and fun. A friend who also has nine children commented, "I don't raise them, I just herd them around." I can relate.

As our family grew, I realized that we needed family home evenings that celebrated the uniqueness of each individual. I searched many books and came across a simple idea. The format we developed we call, "Celebrating the One." We use it for special occasions—birthdays, recovery from illness, leaving on a mission, getting married, and during times of rebellion.

Sometimes we spontaneously select "the one" whom we are celebrating. Other times, the honored one is announced a few days in advance so everyone can prepare. After opening prayer, we go around the room and, with an open heart, share why we love and admire "the one" being honored. Each person takes their turn expressing positive and sincere compliments and insights to "the one." Sometimes special letters, poems, or songs are written to honor "the one." Frequently there is laughter. Always there are tears. In a sweet way, the spirit enters our home during those special occasions in response to sincere expressions of love. In a busy and often cynical world, we frequently fail to speak words of love to those we love the most—our family.

As hearts warm and draw close, we often linger long after the activity is over. Siblings who may have been at odds with one another are laughing, joking, hugging, and apologizing. Defenses and personal walls around hearts melt. Occasionally during these special times, some of us have sensed angels joining us. It may be an unborn child preparing to come to our family or deceased loved ones or others who love us through the veil. They seem to be smiling upon us, joyful at the love and spirit of the Lord fostered by expressions of love.

I share an example of one such home evening. Years ago, when one of our children was struggling through a rebellious phase, we announced I would prepare the rebellious one's favorite dinner, followed by desert at his favorite yogurt store (to ensure he showed up). We had privately spoken to the other children about our concerns for this child and asked them to pray for their sibling during the week before the meeting. We primed the pump by applying a technique Stephen Covey describes in one of his books called Twelve Hugs a Day in which an unhappy or rebellious child receives at least twelve physical or emotional hugs (praise, compliments, thanks) per day.

We had a good week with him, the whole family practicing twelve hugs a day. Some did kind things for him such as making his bed or baking cookies. During the evening of our special meal, we expressed love and praise for him. Later, at the yogurt store, with his brother's arm around him, this young man promised first his brother, and then all of us, that he was ready to change. The miracle was that he did as we continued to shower love and encouragement.

It has become not only an enjoyable practice, but also a sacred home evening tradition in our family to "Celebrate the One." We feel it honors and verifies the power of our Savior's command, "Love one another, as I have loved you" (John 15:12).

Shannon Hoffmann *is a freelance writer and photographer, and also edits the award-winning, national trade publication,* Playground.

★ ★ Keeping Us Together ★ ★

I'VE BEEN A SINGLE PARENT OF THREE sons for the past ten years and editor of *Playground* for the past three and a half years—after going back to school for my B.A. in English. Finishing my degree in the middle of it all has certainly had its challenges, but keeping my family together has been top priority throughout the trial. Our family home evenings have been an important part of achieving both this goal, and that of growing spiritually individually and as a family.

Each of my three sons have favorite family nights, but we all agree that one favorite was a night we actually had home evening with a friend and her sons. She owns a vinyl shop and invited us over to make our own signs. We had a wonderful time choosing favorite sayings and creating our own inspirational artwork. My oldest son, Cedar, gave the lesson from the *Friend*. The lesson was about following the prophet and listening to his teachings to keep us safe from the adversary.

We enjoyed pizza and ice cream after, and the signs grace our home to this day to remind us of that special night, and of course provide inspiration. Not everyone has the same circumstances, and I have come to realize that you never know how much you might enrich someone else's life by sharing these experiences. I think both of our families gained from each other tremendously that evening as my older sons spent time with her two very young sons.

My parents have a wonderful family gathering place we call "The Pond," which has been a favorite place to have family night. We sometimes invite other families there to enjoy it with us as we fish and cook a hot dog or hamburger.

We have adopted many family activities and interests over the years. Another favorite home evening stems from a shared involvement in photography. I shoot photos for magazines, especially the one I edit, and along the way, my sons have all become interested. So one night, we took the camera out, shot sunset photos, and had a lesson on the creation. It was nice to gain a greater appreciation for all Heavenly Father has given for our enjoyment. We had a great discussion about it.

I've always realized the importance of having family home evening, but as my children grow older, participate in more extracurricular activities, and take jobs, it is more difficult to set the same night aside each week. But with the habit established, even if we choose a different evening, we stay close as a family and take time out to learn more about the gospel and become closer to the Lord.

We have also found that family home evening plays an important part in inviting the Spirit to reside in our home.

Emily Warburton Jensen *covers the Bloggernacle (LDS-themed blogs and websites) for the Mormon Times at the Deseret News. She edits both non-fiction and fiction LDS works and misses her time volunteering in the Curriculum Department writing family home evening ideas.*

★ ★ Online Help ★ ★

"Mom! It's time for family home evening? What are we doing?" *What? Time already? Ok, what can I whip into a lesson in say, thirty seconds?* I jump onto my laptop, click into my favorite search engine, type "FHE lesson ideas" and voila! Out streams numerous ideas on a variety of subjects. I skim a few before alighting on one that has a story and explainable activity, and I figure we'll have popsicles for dessert. Wow! What did busy people do before the Internet?

Online are so many handy, creative, fun, spiritual lesson ideas that help to make your family home evening shine, even if you don't have much time to prepare. A few of my favorite resources include the following websites and blogs.

http://nataliesfhespot.blogspot.com/
http://www.ldslivingmagazine.com/categories/show/3
http://fheinasnap.blogspot.com/
http://theideadoor.com/FHE.html
http://fheplanner.blogspot.com/
http://www.jennysmith.net/fhe/100-fhe-ideas.php

Teaching your family about Internet safety is an important family home evening lesson that should be held regularly. Add it to you cadre of lessons on emergency protocol, stranger danger, 72-hour-kits, and so on. In preparing the lesson, check out lds.org. Click on "A-Z Index," then "I" and "Internet" for articles, quotes, and tips on how to approach Internet safety. During the lesson, discuss family rules for the Internet (where the computer is in the home, computer time restraints, filters, and so on). Then explain the real-world dangers of providing your information to those on the Internet and make sure to emphasize to never meet or give anyone your personal information. Discuss the dangers of pornography and how it is important for children to come to you if they have concerns or questions. Finally, discuss the wonderful ways the Internet can bless your home. Enjoy some family Internet time and find some amusing, fun, fascinating, and uplifting activities to do together online.

Bonus lesson: One of my favorite family home evening lessons in recent memory started with everyone taking the time to dress up in best dress (my three little girls love to dress up) and me preparing a stylish tea party complete with juice and cookies on my rose china. As we sat down, I explained the rituals and manners associated with eating in our best dress. I then asked them to think of another place where we respectfully partake of food and should be on our best behavior. My husband provided the answer: the sacrament. We then discussed how lately we have not been on our best behavior during the sacrament and have not used out best manners. We made various comparisons to the tea party and the sacrament and then discussed that if we should be on our best behavior during a tea party, then how much more we should be respectful during the sacrament. It sunk in as I saw a marked change in my children's attitude and quiet respect in the subsequent Sundays.

Daryll M. Jonnson *worked as an international freelance model after graduating from Colorflair Studios and Lascelles School of Deportment, Grooming and Modeling, London, England. She served as President of Christie College, an international business college, and has received the Dale Carnegie Highest Achiever Award. Daryll also founded the fast growing website, LDSWA™ (Latter-day Saint Women's Alliance).*

One Memory Made Home
★ ★ Evenings Work ★ ★

I WAS BORN AND RAISED IN THE United Kingdom, and my parents converted to the Church prior to my eighth birthday. The only time we had family home evening occurred three years later, which shows how important this inspired program is to a child, as the memory is still clear today. Through a fun game, my brother, sister, and I were taught the importance of listening to the whole command and acting upon it instead of choosing to act on one part only.

It was not long after this that my parents separated and later divorced. Because of their divorce, I did not have the opportunity of Church activity for many years, and I eventually married a young man who was not into any type of religion. When I started my family, it became important for me to go back to Church, so I could give my children strong gospel roots.

I faced many obstacles that caused friction in my marriage. Holding FHE was a struggle, but I desperately wanted to do so because of warm feelings experienced during that evening long ago. I knew home evening was important.

For the most part, I arranged family activities that covered up the fact I was trying to teach my children gospel principles. Our marriage disintegrated and I later remarried a man who joined the Church shortly after the wedding. I'm not sure which is harder to live with—a man with no interest in religion or a man weak in his membership who didn't honor his priesthood.

Again, I found the only way to have FHE was to create it around family activities that meant we could all be together and somehow weave a principle into what we were doing in order to leave something of learning and of value for my children. It was hard seeing other families openly bring their family together every week and share this special time together, and hard seeing some good LDS families ignore this important program.

Over the years, I have come to believe that you have to do the best you can in your own circumstances. If it means you can't hold FHE on a Monday evening then another time is fine. Likewise, if you can't prepare and deliver a lesson, or sing a primary song or hymn, then do what you can to take an hour and bring your family together for an activity. To me creating special memories and togetherness is the most important part. I'm not sure my children remember any of our disguised FHE lessons, but watching them in their own lives today, I know some of the principles taught have obviously stayed with them, and for that I am truly thankful.

Now I am married to a wonderful man who honors his Priesthood. We are empty nesters, and I enjoy those evenings where we talk about the gospel and find important principles to learn from our discussions. And you know what? It isn't always on a Monday evening!

If I had my life over again, I'd make many different choices but would never have to choose whether or not to hold family home evening. That would be a given. I hope somewhere in my children's hearts is the type of memory I have of my one and only home evening as a child, which had such a lasting impact on my life.

Tracy Kennick LaPray *won the title of Miss Utah Teen USA in 1989. In 1994, she was Miss Utah USA and one of the top ten runners up in the Miss USA. She has been News Anchor in Southeast Texas as part of the KBMT Channel 12 News family for more than twelve years.*

★ ★ Week-Long Family Nights ★ ★

FAMILY NIGHT SHOULDN'T BE JUST ONCE A WEEK! I know, right now you're thinking this lady's crazy. In fact, the mere thought of having to plan a lesson, scripture, music, activity, and treat more than one night a week is enough to send even the most faithful of followers into a frenzy. Actually, having family night doesn't have to be all of that all the time.

Family lesson time can come at multiple times during the week and we should seize those opportunities whenever we can. For us, it starts the moment my husband walks through the door from work. We all get in a line and sing "Daddy's Homecoming," then the children all run to him for hugs and kisses. That is followed by dinner together and this is often a perfect time for teaching and sharing. We usually begin with everyone sharing the best and worst things about their day. It's a great way for us to learn more about what's happening at school and work, things that might not have been shared otherwise. From there, the conversation often turns to how we can handle future problems. Many times it ends in laughter as we hear the funny things that have happened to one another that day.

Of course, the scheduled family nights are where much of the gospel is learned. However, after much preparation has been put into a lesson, family night with a young family can sometimes seem like a lot of effort with little success. We've all experienced those times when we're trying to give a lesson on the trials of Job even as the baby is spitting up, the one-year-old is crying for a bottle, the three-year-old is fussing because she can't see the pictures, the six-year-old seems more interested in when we can eat the cookies than in the lesson, the dog is whining to be let outside, and the eight-year-old is upset because everyone is being so loud he can't hear the lesson.

We found the key is in not trying to accomplish prolonged lessons that require lengthy sitting. Instead, we pick topics we feel our family needs to work on like sharing or doing service for one another, and then make it an active lesson. We do use the scriptures but we also use pictures, role-play, and plenty of examples. We ask the children to question and comment, which keeps them checked in and participating.

We also incorporate music. Our kids love to sing and run around while the music is playing. It's a positive, good way to finish off the night. We even have a family song—"Let's Be Kind to One Another," which was included in the Church songbook many years ago. My husband's grandmother used to sing it with them. It doesn't matter which one you choose, but having a family song is a great way to bond.

Finally, after the lesson, we challenge our kids to practice what they've learned. If the lesson was on charity, we ask them the next night at dinner if they had a chance to show charity to anyone at school. They try to do one kind thing for someone each day. That way, we keep up with what we talked about all week long, so family night doesn't start and stop on Monday.

Josi S. Kilpack *is the author of seven LDS novels including* Unsung Lullaby, Surrounded by Strangers, *and the Whitney Award winning* Sheep's Clothing. *Her latest book is* Lemon Tart.

★ ★ Healthy Bodies. ★ ★
Healthy Spirits

I'M AFRAID OUR FAMILY HOME EVENINGS AREN'T quite "writable" since we're hit and miss, and often doing a cub scout or young women thing that needs passing off, or delaying until Dad gets home at 7:30 PM, and then forgetting about this homework project and that phone call, and Dad goes in to record the game and gets sucked in a while. I sit down at the computer for JUST ONE MINUTE and *bam!* it's 9:30 and time to berate the kids for staying up too late, and this one says he didn't get any dinner, and that one remembers she has to write a book report, and this one (that's me) wants to go to bed.

The best family home evening we had in the last six months was a lesson on how our bodies work and why we need to treat them with respect. The part that held the children's attention was when I explained in detail the urinary system of the body, why pee is supposed to be light yellow, and how they really need to start flushing the toilet.

After all, caring for both the spiritual and physical sides of our body is important if we are to receive all the blessings Heavenly Father wants to give us.

David Koch *is a painter of traditional western American subjects. His paintings featuring historic pioneer and religious themes are in the Nauvoo Temple and LDS Church publications. David's work was used in Utah's Gubernatorial Inauguration, and one of his paintings was also presented to Vice President Cheney. He recently completed two murals for the House of Representative Chambers in the Utah State Capitol Building*

★ ★ Be Prepared ★ ★

WHEN MY WIFE AND I ASKED OUR kids if they remembered a particular family home evening that was outstanding to them, they immediately mentioned a reward system we initiated called "Kindness Coins."[1] When a family member exhibited a kind act they received a kindness coin, which they could use later to buy prizes.

A few spontaneous activities are nice to do some of the time. We have taken a walk as a family up to the cemetery and looked at gravestones. We found many pioneer headstones, which fostered dialogue about ancestors and trials that other people have faced. This walk also brought up conversation about life after death and the plan of salvation.

Our greatest challenge is being prepared. If we don't plan a weekly home evening objective, then our children get bored. I believe we can use well-prepared home evenings to teach our kids how to live a life of happiness. I recently heard a quote that phrased our charge in a powerful way. We are to pass on "A legacy undiminished."[2] Family home evening is a very good place to accomplish this.

NOTES

1. Karen Finch, *Family Home Evening Games Galore, vol. 2* (Finch Family Games, 1994).

2. Henry B. Eyring, "Ears to Hear," *Ensign*, May 1985, 76.

Laurie (L.C.) Lewis *is the author of* Free Men and Dreamers, vols. 1 and 2: Dark Sky at Dawn *and* Twilight's Last Gleaming. Volume 3, Dawn's Early Light, *coming soon. For seven years, she was a science-education facilitator in the Maryland Carroll County Public School System.*

★ ★ Wiggle Worms ★ ★

MANY NIGHTS, WE COULD NOT HAVE BEEN convicted of having held family home evening based on what people would have seen if they peeked through our curtains. Ours were generally not the reverent everyone-sitting-with-their-arms-folded kind of family home evening of which mothers and fathers dream. Often, we settled for just being all together, not always at home, not always for a lesson, and sometimes even attending a child's ball game.

Tom and I were both converts, and we really winged it through the early days. I remember making home evening packets from *Ensign* articles and using stories from the *Friend*, and from lessons in the old home evening manual, but our children primarily remember the flannel board set of lessons. We hung a blanket over a chair and watched as everyone took turns making a story unfold from one of the many packets of flannel-backed figures.

Our children also remember the summer we read the entire Book of Mormon together. Struggling through a verse at a time, we even whispered the words into the ears of the three-year-old so he too could repeat the words and "read" with the family. I clearly remember my mega-lesson on the Tree of Life. I spent hours stringing a rope "iron rod" maze, hanging bunches of grapes in a tree and cranking up the pool filter to resemble the "fountain of filthy water," but interestingly, only one child vaguely remembers it now.

Again, after polling our children, a few facts became clear. Very few specific lessons were remembered. What they did recall vividly were the feelings. Perhaps it was the very spirit of excitement of the anticipated "event" that made them especially wiggly, as if they knew that something special was about to happen. They loved the assignment chart, giving each child the opportunity to shine in different capacities, and they loved the treat. Perhaps there is an important spiritual principle even in that seemingly temporal portion of family night—after the sacrifice of time and obedience comes the reward.

In hindsight, one of the most enduring rewards of FHE came from our little family councils when we'd go around the room, detailing upcoming events, activities, or challenges each family member would face in the coming week. The few focused moments spent on each person provided a platform to highlight them and their achievements and afforded us the opportunity to rally support to whoever needed it. Appreciation, family pride, and a spirit of gratitude were all fostered by that simple exercise, and as a result, our children's self-esteem flourished. One of the things that most delights me now is the continued support our children provide to one another. Though all are out of the house and scattered from coast to coast, they communicate with one another almost daily, by phone, email, or through our family web site.

It is charming to me now, that our wiggle worms, who so frequently disrupted the reverence of family home evening, have become diligent about holding it in their own homes. I know our meager efforts to be obedient were magnified by the Spirit. Even today, the favorite parts of Lewis gatherings are family devotionals and home evening lessons that spring from family love and a love of the Lord. This was long ago etched upon the hearts of wriggling children, sitting cross-legged before blankets dotted with flannel-board figures, and in the simple activities we shared together.

Patty Liston *is the Director of Women's Initiatives for Reach the Children and also works for Children's Way as their Director of Partnerships. She is a writer, speaker, and teacher, and has cohosted two radio shows. Patty travels to Africa yearly to participate in humanitarian work with Reach the Children.*

★ ★ Finding Pieces ★ ★

A S I WALKED THROUGH THE VILLAGE OF Kiamumbi, just outside Nairobi, Kenya, goats and chickens pecked along beside me while little children ran up yelling the only English they knew, "How are you?" I laughed and bent to hug them, replying that I was fine.

For as long as I could remember, Africa stood as a reminder of a premortal life promise, its echo reaching me in my stillness. A part of me always knew this country held pieces of me that would be found in moments of simplicity and wonder.

This was my first trip as a volunteer with Reach the Children, an organization working toward self-sustainable development in the villages and slums of Africa. We had spent the day teaching at an elementary school when Njenga, the headmaster, asked if we would like to see the village. I was eager to meet the mothers and walked through the dust that led me to a woman who unknowingly held a piece of me.

She sat on a small ledge holding a baby wrapped in a thin woven blanket that burst with the red, black, and yellow colors of Kenya. She smiled shyly as I said hello and asked if I could see her baby. She gently exposed her child's face and I gazed into wide, dark chocolate brown eyes. I asked his name. "Joseph," she said. "I named him after my prophet, Joseph Smith."

I couldn't speak as images and words surfaced and tumbled forcefully through my mind; of a fourteen-year-old boy kneeling in a grove of trees. Over a century of time distanced that Joseph to *this* child, *this*

Joseph of Africa. Tears filled my eyes as I felt the divine orchestration of this moment when two women, divided by an ocean of differences and opportunities, would meet on common gospel ground, "as sisters in Zion." Wrapping my arms around mother and child, I shared that I too was a member of The Church of Jesus Christ of Latter-day Saints.

My new sister asked if I would like to see her home. She held Joseph and placing her slim dark hand into my white freckled one, we walked the narrow dirt ally that led to her home. Hers was the last of a row of corrugated metal sheds. She parted the worn red cloth that kept the dust from her threshold, and I stepped into the dark. A table holding a few wooden bowls and utensils stood at the center, with a wooden chair arranged neatly on either side. This was the only furniture. Plastic sheets I knew served as beds were rolled in a corner. This room, and two areas off it, housed eleven. She said we stood in the room where all of them sat for family home evening. Here they sang songs they loved and taught the children the gospel of Jesus Christ.

I imagined eleven people sitting together on the plastic sheets to share the gospel. I knew there would be no visual aids, scriptures, or treats, but the spirit bore witness to me that here, on the dirt floor, truth was taught, testimonies born, revelation given, and the Spirit invited in. I never felt more humbled and knew I would never again be the same. As we hugged good-bye, I couldn't believe I'd lived my life without knowing her. Now, she would always be a part of it. She was my piece. As I walked back to the school, I realized it was Monday—family home evening night. I thought of her family gathered together, learning to keep the commandments. Dozens of small children walked along beside me laughing and yelling, "How are you?" I smiled and thought, *I'm fine. Oh, I am fine.*

Dr. Kelly Loosli *has spent seventeen years in the film and animation industries including working for both DreamWorks Feature Animation and Buena Vista Motion Pictures at Disney. He obtained a BA in Film from Brigham Young University and received a Student Emmy for his clay-animated film,* Nocturnal. *Kelly teaches BYU courses in Traditional Animation, Storyboarding, and senior year film development.*

★ ★ Cowboy Home Evening ★ ★

I GREW UP IN A SUPER LDS family, most of who came from farming communities in Idaho. They were a little rougher than your average Mormon these days.

One Monday, when I was about five or six and still thought cowboys were cool, my two younger brothers and I found out about Dad growing up on a farm and that he knew how to lasso cattle.

We quickly went and got whatever rope we had lying around and convinced my dad to lasso us as part of family home evening. For approximately two hours, my brothers and I ran back and forth in front of an empty wall in our living room while dad lassoed us. He caught our feet with the rope, pulled, and we fell, laughing ourselves silly. After this, we wrapped up the evening with our usual treats and prayer.

Once a month we got together for home evening with my mom's side of the family and once a month with my dad's. It was great as we got to know extended family so well. Usually, these home evenings were casual, but sometimes my grandfather on my mother's side (who ended up giving me my patriarchal blessing as well as performing my sealing in the temple) would give a great talk on subjects like the Atonement or a challenge to read specific *Ensign* articles. However, to this day, playing cowboys with Dad still comes first in my memory.

James Bryan Loynes *was born in Wales and currently lives in Southport, England. His fine baritone voice can be heard on BBC radio and at BBC live stage tours. He also sings on British national television. James and his wife, Francesca, founded United Voice, a choir of a hundred-plus, which performs in the country's top concert venues including the Royal Liverpool Philharmonic Hall and the Cathedral at Blackburn, Lancashire. James runs his own school of music where he is a vocal coach. He recently worked with LDS songwriter Sally Deford to produce a Christmas album,* His Name Shall Be Called Wonderful.

★ ★ Becoming Close ★ ★

GROWING UP, FAMILY HOME EVENING OFTEN SEEMED difficult to pull off. Each family member was strong-willed, with something to say. We seemed to have explosive chemistry that often brought the whole thing to a close, leaving us unenthusiastic—even for refreshments!

We sometimes made the mistake of trying to be too formal with our family nights and were disappointed when not everyone took everything seriously. We needed something a bit different to a Sunday School class, something to accommodate restless personalities with the urge to offer our two pennies worth!

In the end, the greatest home evenings weren't those when someone stood up and lectured about a gospel principle, but when we all had the opportunity to talk about what the principle meant to us and how it made each of us feel. This kind of lively discussion helped us understand each other.

We think we know our family members better than anyone because we live under the same roof, but there's so much more we can discover about each other. As a collector finds new pieces, he loves his collection more and more. As a scholar stumbles across new information, he loves his subject more. It's the same with families. The more we find out, the closer we become.

Fun get-to-know-you games, both spiritual and just plain silly, are a great way to enjoy each family member's personality and unique take on life. The following are examples of questions to ask.

- ★ What's your sister's favorite scripture?
- ★ What's your brother's favorite hymn?
- ★ Who baptized your mom?
- ★ If your dad could be a Disney character, who would he be?
- ★ What makes your grandma really laugh?

Now that I'm married to Francesca, it's easy to fall into the trap of thinking, "We're always together, just the two of us," and not seeing family night as necessary. Of course, that isn't true. It's so important that we set aside time where we stop the routine and keep rediscovering the gospel and how it is affecting both of our lives. Family home evening for newlyweds can be like taking a spiritual inventory at the same time as gaining a better understanding of each other.

Since both Francesca and I love good music, and we understand how it can influence harmony in the home, we hope that when we have children, it will be one more thing the Loynes family will share during family night that will help keep us close.

Dr. John L. Lund *is a motivational presenter to CEOs and corporate managers across the country. He was also cofounder of Frontier Pies Restaurants and Bakery, Inc. He holds three certifications as an Arbitrator, Mediator, and a Negotiator, and has taught as adjunct faculty at major universities throughout Washington, Idaho, California, and Utah. His latest book is* How To Hug A Porcupine: Dealing With Toxic And Difficult to Love Personalities.

The Best Thing I Ever
★ ★ Did as a Parent ★ ★

RAISING EIGHT CHILDREN REQUIRES EIGHT DIFFERENT PARENTING plans. It also requires a considerable amount of prayer. The great lesson I learned as a parent was to take my love to my family and my frustration about my family to the Lord. It is easy as a parent to be frustrated and upset because our expectations aren't being met, and to become a "critiholic." This doesn't mean there is not a time and a place for appropriate criticism; there is (see D&C 121:43). It means we need to be sparing in the amount of negative messages we are sending to any particular child, whether they are eighteen months or eighteen years of age, or else our words "I love you" fall on deaf ears, and we wind up with a child who believes we are their enemy.

If I can only criticize rarely, how can I deal with the misbehaving child? First, make sure you are sending more positive messages than negative ones. Most experts recommend a five to one ratio. That means five positive messages for every negative message we send.

Here is one way to send a positive message. Give each child a twenty minute one-on-one positive home evening sharing time each week. It requires scheduling and a commitment on the part of the parent. I met with my eight children on Monday night, eight twenty-minute sessions. My wife would take one-one-one time with a different child a day (with two children on one day to fit in all eight). I considered it a sacred commitment, and I would not take phone calls nor allow anything to interfere with the "Positive Sharing Time." This sent a message to the children that they were important. It was a commitment I kept while serving twice as a bishop and once in a Stake Presidency. My wife would inform the seeker of my time that I was in a counseling session and would not be available until 10:00 PM.

What did we do during the twenty minutes of sharing time? We played Candyland, chess, or some other age appropriate game, and talked about things that were important to them. It was not a time to lecture, preach, or rebuke. Those occasions were part of another session. This was a positive experience and a time for me as a parent to get into their world. It was a time to read Dr. Seuss' *Green Eggs and Ham* with the four-year-old and to answer questions about the scriptures with the young man preparing to leave on a mission. It was an opportunity to assure a fourteen-year-old girl that you too had pimples when you were fourteen and that this too would pass. When it was time to share twenty minutes with one of the babies, I would just hold them, put them on my shoulders, or sing to them. These were times for me as a parent to enter their world, not bring them into the adult world. It was a time for bonding and positive interaction and it was consistent. Rarely in twenty-five years of parenting did I miss that special time with each of the children.

Was I a perfect parent? No. Did I make mistakes? Yes. I could write a book on my mistakes. However, having a weekly one-on-one positive sharing time with each child for twenty minutes is one of those things that say, "I love you." Family home evening, family prayer, and reading the scriptures are a part of a great program to develop unity and to teach the gospel. Without question, those one-on-one sessions were the best things I ever did as a parent.

Annette Lyon *is Utah's 2007 Best of State Fiction Medalist and the best-selling LDS author of several books, including the historical novels* House on the Hill, At the Journey's End, *and her newest book, a retelling of a Shakespeare favorite:* Spires of Stone, *a 2007 Whitney Award finalist for best historical novel.* Tower of Strength *is the next volume.*

★ ★ Two for the Price of One ★ ★

BETWEEN CUB SCOUTS, BOY SCOUTS, DUTY TO God, and Faith in God, our children have so many things they need to pass off that it sometimes gets overwhelming. We've found that using family home evening as a chance to pass off some items for these programs works well.

Service projects, scripture reading and discussions, musical and cultural experiences, teaching lessons, reading from the general conference reports, memorizing the Articles of Faith, and more are all requirements that can be easily adapted to family home evening with little preparation but big results.

We recently spent several weeks going through the For the Strength of Youth pamphlet during home evening, covering two or three topics each week. We read a section, the associated scripture, and then discussed what it meant to us and why it was important to live by those values. It was a wonderful opportunity to recommit our family to the standards and to explain to the younger children why those principles are so important.

Jill C. Manning, *PhD, is a Licensed Marriage & Family Therapist who specializes in clinical work related to pornography and problematic sexual behavior. She is the author of* What's the Big Deal about Pornography: A Guide for the Internet Generation, *and has been featured in television programs, documentaries, and radio talk shows.*

Family Home Evening as a Couple:
A Practice that Fosters an Intentional Marriage

"WHAT DO I MEAN BY AN INTENTIONAL marriage? It's one where the partners are conscious, deliberate, and planful about maintaining and building their commitment and connection over the years. They see themselves as active citizens of their marriage rather than passive consumers."[1]

Having worked as a marriage and family therapist, I've learned firsthand that solid marriages and families are never accidental—they reflect years of intentional acts that are in harmony with gospel living. When my husband, Michael, and I married in 2006, we made a commitment that we wanted to start many of those intentional acts from the start, in order to lay strong foundation for our future children and family. Holding weekly family home evening as a couple was one such practice we were committed to implementing right from the start. How we have come to cherish those weekly meetings! Family night affords us the opportunity to set the world aside and to nurture our marriage relationship in unique and deliberate ways. When we hold family home evening, we feel an increased measure of the Spirit in our home, increased love for one another, and heightened attunement to each other's needs and lives—not to mention we have fun!

In our home, we each take turns selecting a message, activity, or focus for the evening. Turn taking has been a great way to learn about each other's talents, strengths, testimony, and interests. I've come to appreciate Michael's passion for the scriptures and the words of our modern-day prophets, as well as his talents in music. He, on the other hand, has learned about my love for uplifting stories, doing physical activities together as a family, playing games, and reading books that focus on how to strengthen marriage and family relationships, including *The Seven Principles for Making Marriage Work,* by John Gottman, and *Rock Solid Relationships: Strengthening Personal Relationships with Wisdom from the Scriptures,* by Wendy L. Watson.

We also incorporated something we call Marriage Maintenance into our weekly home evenings. The name, Marriage Maintenance, is a spin-off of the health maintenance visits my husband conducts with patients in his medical practice. Marriage Maintenance gives both of us an opportunity to check-in with one another and share what the upcoming week will look like; discuss how we can support each other with specific assignments, goals, or demands; identify problems that need to be tackled; and review how our marriage relationship may be strengthened. We find this practice also creates a space and time in which we can express appreciation and gratitude for things we may have neglected to express during the week. When children become part of future home evenings, we are committed to moving Marriage Maintenance to another time each week, since neither of us wants to end this valuable practice.

Although family home evening will change and bring forth new meaning (and certainly new challenges) when our children come, we know that this tradition and practice will work for our family's good if we are diligent in our efforts and simply do our best to make it an enriching experience. For now, family home evening is something that strengthens our new marriage and invites the Lord's mentoring influence into our newly formed family. We are most grateful for this prophetic and inspired practice.

NOTE

1. William J. Doherty, Ph.D., *Take Back Your Marriage: Sticking Together in a World that Pulls Us Apart,* 18.

Kelly Martinez *is a writer who has worked for the* Los Angeles Times, *the* Long Beach Press-Telegram, *and the* Deseret Morning News. *He worked in the collegiate sports information field since 1992 and was a member of the Los Angeles Clippers' stat crew from 1995–99. He is currently the sports editor for* Meridian Magazine.

★ ★ It Worked. After All ★ ★

AWKWARD WOULD PROBABLY BE THE BEST WORD to describe the times my mother called us around for a formal family night involving a song, lesson, and prayer. When my mother announced it was time for home evening, she was met with rolling eyes and bad attitudes from my brother and me. We had other things we'd rather be doing than sitting through another Church lesson. Eventually, my mom gave up and the lessons stopped. Our Monday nights were ours again to selfishly indulge in whatever fun we could find.

From September to December, for instance, Monday nights involved Monday Night Football (MNF), homemade burritos, and macaroni and cheese. Our family would help make dinner together and then gather around the TV in time for kickoff. Howard Cosell's "Halftime Highlights" and "Dandy" Don Meredith's singing "Turn out the lights, the party's over" at the end of each game were family favorites. Intermingled with the game, we discussed how we were doing in school, our upcoming Church assignments, our extended family members, current events, and gospel-related topics.

When the MNF season was over, Monday nights involved miniature golfing, movies, drives along the southern California coast, trips to the park, trips to the beach, and other activities. Although I didn't realize at the time, family night had evolved from Church-like lessons to other family strengthening activities. It was family home evening in disguise! Gone were the formal lessons, but the bonding and strengthening of our family were still intact. With each of the activities came lessons and discussions on things such as honesty, missions, marriage, dating, tithing, and whatever other topic mom had in mind to discuss that week.

I admire my mom's ability to turn family night from something her family was less than enthusiastic about into something that truly strengthened family bonds.

Fast forward to when my own children were young. My wife and I were determined to make family night a priority in our home. Home evening involved a song, a prayer, a lesson, and refreshments. It was easier to do when our sons were little; they loved taking their turns leading the songs and giving the lessons. As they grew into teenagers, however, formal lesson-based home evenings have fallen by the wayside. Family night now is more like the ones I remember when my mom "gave up" on FHE.

Mostly, our family nights involve activities like concerts, movies, and sporting events. As our oldest son nears adulthood, it is difficult to keep him involved because of his busy schedule with a job and other school-related activities. But we are blessed enough to gather as a family at least once a week and spend time together.

I don't think there is a clear-cut answer to the "how" aspect of FHE. For a long time, I felt as if I was failing at the whole thing. It took me a while to realize that it has played a big and influential role in my life all along. From my childhood years to the present, family nights have helped me draw nearer to those I love and am blessed enough to call my family.

Carlos Martins *from Brazil is owner and president of the Wizard chain of schools, which are renowned for teaching English and other languages throughout his own country, and in the United States, Japan, and Europe. Wizard is also the only language school in Brazil offering English courses in Braille.*

★ ★ Put Them in Charge ★ ★

I WAS TWELVE YEARS OLD WHEN MY parents joined The Church of Jesus Christ of Latter-day Saints. They were looking for a church to help them raise their seven children. After our baptism, the branch president in Curitiba, Brazil, did all he could to fellowship our family in the gospel. We went to his house and he showed us how to hold a family home evening. We were grateful for his love and concern and for setting us an example as new converts.

One night, while my wife and I were on our honeymoon, we sat on the sand of a beautiful beach in Brazil and held our first family home evening. That night we made some important goals for our new family that we still strive to keep to this day.

The Lord blessed us with six children. When our four oldest children were still at home was the time we found most challenging to hold home evening on a consistent basis. It seemed everyone was involved in some important activity. Whenever we tried to get them all together, it seemed their schedules would not match. Then we had some inspiration. Why not let each child conduct a family night one week of the month?

We proposed this to the children and to our surprise, they gladly accepted. We were amazed to see how their reaction to home evening changed. The moment they became responsible for the planning, lessons, assignments, organization, scheduling, refreshments, and activities, we no longer had problems with conflicting interests competing with FHE. Their spirit of cooperation, involvement, and participation improved significantly. As we look back this was indeed a very inspired thought.

Children often ask parents to do something, go somewhere, participate in some activity, or bring friends over. Sometimes these requests come at a time when parents cannot give children their full attention. Maybe the issue might demand some extra consideration. With this in mind, my wife and I decided we would not discuss some of these issues immediately with the children. We established a rule that we would deal with important family decisions during family home evening. Sometimes, when one of their requests was a little surprising, through the spirit in home evening, the children came to their own conclusion as to why a certain course of action should not be followed.

When our oldest sons married, we had two teenage daughters and our smaller sons at home. It was difficult to have a common message or activity that would please both age groups. So we agreed to start the meeting together as a family. After the hymn and prayer, the next fifteen minutes would be specifically for the small ones. They could then leave if they wanted to and we would change the focus to the interests of the teenagers. That way, we could accommodate the needs of the little ones and at the same time show concern for our teenagers.

We have a strong testimony of the benefits of family night. We know this is something the Lord has provided to help us become a celestial family.

Jeanne McKinney *is a maverick writer and filmmaker. Her work has won recognition, screenings, and awards across the U.S. and Canada. She's written eleven screenplays, including the epic animated trilogy,* Eagle Warrior™, *and her latest co-authored work,* The Ardanea Pendant, *winning First Prize (IFFF 2008) and Best New Writer finalist (AOF 2008).*

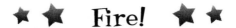 Fire!

S OMETHING FROM WHICH MY FAMILY BENEFITED WAS a personal Emergency Response course. My husband taught us how to best react when helping people in trouble with sudden health issues, trauma, accidents, and so forth. He had taken a course through his work where he became certified and passed the knowledge on to us. Practicing on each other is a good family home evening activity. It can be part of an emergency preparedness family plan, along with food and water storage.

As a family, we've gone through two major wildfires here in California and experienced an emergency response involving millions of people of all ages and health conditions. It's good to know basic emergency procedures, which can help save a life, or at least not complicate the situation until a emergency response team arrives. Hospitals and medical personnel are on high alert during these times. One entire hospital was evacuated during the biggest of the ten fires (the Witch Fire), in October 2007, causing an overload on other facilities. Some areas lost all power, which hindered medical treatment in some cases. Knowing how to best treat acute emergency situations comes in handy for oneself, one's family, and others in need.

Marcia Mickelson, *originally from Guatemala, is the author of three published LDS novels,* Star Shining Brightly, Reasonable Doubt, *and* Pickup Games

Family Home Evening
★ ★ in the Car ★ ★

AFTER THE ANNOUNCEMENT THAT A TEMPLE WOULD be built in San Antonio, Texas, our family took the opportunity to follow its progress. We spent many family home evenings driving to the temple to see how construction was progressing.

Our children were four and two. At that age, home evening was often chaotic and challenging since small kids do not want to sit still for long. However, we found they did in the car. After all, they were strapped in, and couldn't get up and wander away as they could at home. While in the car, we listened to children's hymn during the twenty-minute drive. Other times, we listened to CDs of the primary sacrament meeting program given to us by our ward's primary presidency. It helped the children practice the songs they were learning in primary. We also read scriptures in the car. The children were usually good during this time since there were no distractions. Sometimes, we took our portable DVD player and they watched Book of Mormon video stories on the way.

At the temple site, we pointed out changes since the last time we were there. We explained what the temple was and why it was important. Often, we would run into other families who were there for the same reason and shared our excitement in having a temple so close. We took many pictures of our kids in front of the temple documenting different stages of construction. To cap off the night, we had our traditional chocolate milk shakes. Sometimes, we made them at home and had them on the way to the temple. Other times, we stopped and bought them. I doubt our family will ever forget the good feelings we took away each time we visited the temple grounds.

Sherry Ann Miller *is an award-winning author, and is also known as the "Writer of Miracles." Her books include the five-book Gift Series, the two-book* Warwick Saga, Mama's Lemon Pie, *and many more.*

★ ★ A Most Important Thing ★ ★

Family night was intended to be the most important evening of the week. Knowing this to be true, my husband and I agreed early in our marriage that family home evening would occur on Monday night without fail. Nothing stood in its way except a dire emergency (such as a broken leg occurring within an hour or two of the event). Church activities, school activities, telephone calls, television, and the Internet were not allowed to interfere with home evening.

Everyone in our ward, and within the circles of our children's friends, knew if they called on Monday night, someone from the household would answer, "Hello, it's family home evening at the Miller's house." People learned not to call the Miller's after 6:00 PM on Mondays. Either that or the children were so mortified, they warned their friends not to try.

Each week, we assigned and prepared a topic. The kids thought of ways to make refreshments and activities relate to the lesson topic. Many of them "traded" lesson assignments with each other when they were in seminary, after learning something they were dying to share.

We later heard that children were more likely to follow the gospel if family night was held regularly. Today, our children are grown and we have twenty-seven grandchildren. We can see the love they have for one another and realize their family-oriented lifestyles were nurtured during family nights. We're glad we took it seriously from the beginning.

Patti Miner *is a former Mrs. Utah America and has three college degrees. She has taught school, and has filmed and voiced commercials, industrial films, and movies. Patti recorded four CDs, winning Top Video and New Country Female Artist awards, and was nominated for Best Songwriter. Author of four books, she has lectured throughout the U.S. Patti also co-owned and operated a Model and Talent Agency, was National Public Spokesperson for "For Kids Sake," and State Public Spokesperson for the Red Cross. She worked with underprivileged children in "The Kid Konnection" and "The Christmas Box House."*

✦ ✦ Adapting Through the Years ✦ ✦

WHEN THE CHILDREN WERE YOUNGER, WE HAD regular family home evenings. As a former school teacher, I had visual aids and puppets we could use to teach concepts. All the kids remember and still laugh about the puppet shows because we had a stage made from cardboard and the children helped make puppets. They changed their voices and added their own music.

At first, we parents taught the lessons, but as the children grew older they became excited to teach their younger siblings, who in turn now teach our grandchildren.

Before we had the professional home evening book with Church guidelines, we used the missionary "Gospel Principles" book as a lesson manual, making it fun with treats, songs, games, and activities.

One year we each shared and taught our talents. Dad and the boys taught a variety of sports, the girls taught dancing, and mom singing. We had fun but also appreciated how difficult each talent was. Another year, the focus was Emergency Preparedness and Learning Life Skills. One lesson was on first aid. We laugh now at photos of the children wrapping each other up like mummies with bandages. However, two of my children, each at different times and later in life, actually won awards for life saving skills taught that day.

One lesson was on starting our scrapbooks, which we continue to update twice a year as a general conference tradition. I recently called my daughter on a conference Saturday, and she and her daughters were doing their scrapbooks. I hung up the phone teary-eyed with memories of my children and joy seeing at that tradition continued.

Family home evenings evolved from a regular time on Monday night when the children were young—to Sunday evenings when children had sports or lessons on Monday. At one point, as a busy mother and professional woman with busy children all pursuing talents, we had irregular family home evenings on different nights. We discussed schedules at Sunday dinner to see when everyone could get together.

As the children grew and had their own families, we had dinner every Sunday afternoon. One great home evening was when we took turns sharing about their missions. They brought scrapbooks, videos, and told many amazing faith promoting stories. These days, we try scheduling something once a month with the ones close by, such as camping, or trips to the zoo, or trips to amusement parks. I believe we can enjoy each season of life if we do our best to incorporate the teachings of the Church and follow the Spirit in our individual family situations. The bottom line is that children grow up knowing their parents have a testimony and love the Lord.

Heather B. Moore *is the Whitney Award winning author of the* Out of Jerusalem series: Of Goodly Parents, A Light in the Wilderness, Towards the Promised Land, *and* Land of Inheritance. *The first book in her new series is* Abinadi, *the 2008 Whitney Award Winner for Best Historical Fiction and 2009 Best of State Winner in Literary Arts for Historical Fiction. Heather's next book is titled* Alma the Elder.

★ ★ Fun Games ★ ★

AS A YOUNG MOTHER, I WAS IN a FHE group where we each made cute lessons and then traded them around with the group. My young children loved to play the games, listen to the short story, and make the correlating treat. I used those FHE lessons as part of primary lessons or primary talks for my children as well.

But as my children grew older, we needed a change. And I seemed to have less and less time to prepare for FHE. Especially when I started writing, many of the smaller things went out the window. We started using the *Friend* magazines. I'd have one child pick a story for the night, and my husband or I would read it. Then we'd all discuss the theme or the scripture that went with the story. We'd let a different child choose a primary song to sing, then we'd play our traditional game—"the animal game."

It's quite silly, really, but my kids always begged to play it. Each person (adult or child) takes a turn acting out an animal. And the first person to guess what it is gets to go next. Now lest you think our children acted out a dog or cat, I'd have to correct you. Because our children frequently watched the Discovery channel, we parents were quite stumped many times. And then the youngest child, of course, would either copy the child right before her or do something very un-animal-like. Regardless, everyone got a good laugh. And the very simple and hardly-planned evening ended with family prayer.

Sometimes we'd change it up a little. A child would choose a picture from the Gospel Art Kit, and a parent would read the story on the back. We'd paraphrase for the younger ones, or look up scriptures with the older ones. If the story was right, we'd let the kids act it out. One of my kids' favorites is when Ammon offers to be a servant in King Lamoni's court. My kids like to pretend they're fighting the sheep-robbers, then lie as if dead on the floor of the king's palace.

We used another idea when our children had talk assignments in church. During family night, the child rehearsed the talk. Or if a primary program was coming up, we'd have the children go over a few of the songs in family home evening.

You can't go wrong with simple stories, songs, a few scriptures, and games.

Dr. Lloyd D. Newell *has addressed audiences around the world as a professional speaker and has worked as a television news anchor. Since 1990 he has written and announced the Mormon Tabernacle Choir's weekly broadcast, "Music and the Spoken Word." Dr. Newell teaches classes at BYU for Religious Education and the School of Family Life, and is the author of numerous books, including the best-selling daily devotional book,* Let Him Ask of God.

⭐ ⭐ Blessed for Trying ⭐ ⭐

THE FAMILY HOME EVENING PROGRAM OF THE Church continues to bless our family every week. Like you, we've have good family nights and bad ones, amazing ones and dreadful ones. While it's not always a powerful or transcendent experience, regular family home evening, over time, strengthens and enhances the spirit in our home. It unites us as a family. In a sometimes turbulent world, family night is something steady and reliable. As we've persisted in our efforts, family home evening has become a habit, a consistent spiritual pattern. It provides regular opportunities for us to laugh and sing, to have a treat and fun activity, and most importantly, to focus on gospel principles— together as a family. The promised blessings and rich rewards of regular family home evening sometimes are not immediate, but they continue to inspire our best efforts. And when we do experience the sweetness of family night, we are motivated to work through the rough spots.

Unfortunately, too many families are paralyzed by a picture of perfection that they've never seen but somehow think is happening in other families: "Other families don't argue during family night." "Other children sit reverently and participate cheerfully." "Other families have well-planned lessons every week. What's wrong with us?"

No family is perfect. If we were, we wouldn't need spiritual patterns like family home evening to help us through mortality. If we give up because of our family's shortcomings, then we're missing the point of family home evening—to make imperfect families stronger. Failed attempts, instead of discouraging us, should reaffirm to us the need to keep trying.

The First Presidency, noting "evidence of the corrosive elements targeted to injure our youth" and expressing deep concern for those "who fall into the adversary's net and drift into inactivity," counseled families to "give highest priority to family prayer, family home evening, gospel study and instruction, and wholesome family activities. However worthy and appropriate other demands or activities may be, they must not be permitted to displace the divinely-appointed duties that only parents and families can adequately perform."[1]

It's those other "worthy and appropriate" demands that sometimes present the biggest obstacle. An informal survey asked more than 100 BYU students about family home evening and other spiritual patterns in the families in which they grew up. The students said that when these patterns were disrupted, it wasn't because of what we might consider serious family challenges, such as divorce or abusive behavior. It was for more mundane reasons, like school activities, work schedules, athletics, television shows, and homework. Busy lives, filled with competing "good" commitments, were the main reason spiritual patterns faltered.

What can we do to keep other activities from creeping in and taking precedence over weekly family home evening?

One key is to be creative and adapt family home evening to the ages and stages of family members. Family home evening for teenage children with demanding homework loads may be a well-planned twenty minutes. For smaller children it may be even shorter. The length of time is not as important as the consistent bonding that family home evening can provide when given priority and held regularly.

Another important element is to establish a regular time and place for family home evening. This way, when other activities come up, they must be scheduled around the time set aside for family home evening—not the other way around. When as a family we have clearly outlined the expectations, family members more readily embrace the habit.

Despite our careful planning, however, disruptions and lapses may occur. But having a plan in place makes it easier to get back on track, especially if we develop the plan together as a family. When each family member participates in establishing expectations, family members can remind each other of our commitment and help each other achieve our common goal.

Of course, one of the reasons we obey the counsel to hold family night is because we hope for certain outcomes for our families—more understanding of the plan of salvation, more unity, increased love for one another, greater faith and strength to resist temptation. But we can't force these outcomes; we can only do our best and trust the Lord's promises. And when children resist our honest efforts, we must remember that sincerity and love are the greatest motivators, not force and fury.

In all of this, we also remember that the Lord will bless us for trying, for doing our best to obey, even if the outcome isn't always what we had hoped. He is aware of our offerings of time and energy in behalf of our families. To all who make earnest effort, the Lord said, "[Your] sacrifice shall be more sacred unto me than [your] increase" (D&C 117:13). In the Lord's sight, effort is sacred, and our families deserve our best efforts.

NOTE

1. First Presidency, Letter to the members of the Church, Feb. 11, 1999; see "Policies, Announcements, and Appointments," *Ensign,* June 1999, 80.

Rachel Ann Nunes *is the best-selling author of over two dozen novels, including the Ariana Series,* Winter Fire, Flying Home, Fields of Home, *and* Eyes of a Stranger. *Her novel* The Independence Club *was a finalist for the 2007 Whitney Award in the Romance/ Women's Fiction category, and her novel* Fields of Home *won a Whitney Award for Best General Fiction, 2008. She has also published two award-winning picture books,* Daughter of a King *and* The Secret of the King.

Learning Obedience
★ ★ from Paper ★ ★

ONE OF OUR FAMILY'S MOST MEMORABLE FAMILY home evenings happened when we took our six children, then ages four to seventeen, to a park that has a playground and a lake filled with ducks. We bought pizza and root beer to eat there, and donuts for dessert. Our feast began attracting many flies, but we all agreed to make the best of dinner anyway. We kept our cups covered with napkins and joked about catching flies with soda.

While we finished eating, we let the little ones run around to use up some of their boundless energy. Spirits were high and the noise level, too. But there were only two falls and one "He hit me" before it was time to sit on the blanket for our lesson.

First, I talked about the importance of striving to obey the commandments of the Lord with faith and exactness and how being obedient to those who have stewardship over us will help us not only in our spiritual but also temporal lives. I retold the story of the stripling warriors who, because of the faithful obedience taught to them by their mothers, were able to be strong and worthy soldiers and have their lives miraculously preserved. Their faith in God allowed them to show exact obedience to their leader (Alma 57:21).

Then, while I passed out paper, my husband made a paper airplane. He showed it to the children and asked them to make an airplane like his. Some of the older children succeeded in making a plane, though not

112

nearly as nice as his, but the younger ones were helpless. He explained that if they listened carefully, he could teach them to make his special airplane. Everyone was eager! So fold by fold, my husband showed the children how to make his plane, stressing the importance of following each direction or commandment with exactness.

The children who listened ended up with airplanes that flew high and far. A few had to redo their planes, asking for individual help from Dad. How simple it was when they followed each direction with exactness, just as our lives are easier when we follow the commandments of the Lord!

Afterwards, we tried feeding the ducks, but they weren't hungry. Fortunately, some mean-looking geese greedily ate up everything we'd brought. Only one child ended up knee deep in the lake. There was a lot of laughter as we played together. We finished the evening by watching the smaller kids on the playground while we chatted with our older children.

Not all our family nights have been so successful and fun—in fact, some nights we've experienced what I feel is more than our share of discouragement—but we understand that by striving to follow the Lord's commandment to gather our family, we will open ourselves for more evenings like these—evenings that make disastrous attempts worth the effort.

I know my children will probably forget the lesson we had that day, and even the reason we flew the planes, but they won't forget being together and the love we shared. That closeness will leave them willing to learn about the gospel as nothing else can.

Dr. Terrance D. Olson *is a professor in the School of Family Life at BYU and former associate director of the World Family Policy Center. He has written programs for public schools, published in professional and church periodicals, and helped edit the* Encyclopedia of Mormonism. *He is a fellow of the Wheatley Institution at BYU.*

Family Home Evening Begins in Our Hearts: ★ ★ Giving faith. hope. and charity a chance ★ ★

IT IS UNDERSTANDABLE HOW SOME OF US approach family home evening with a feeling of being burdened by the whole idea. Yet that very attitude often contributes to the problem. Family home evening can take on the spirit we bring to it. If we dread the event, what signals are we sending to our children? Imperfect people may rarely produce perfect home evenings, but we can create and deliver meaningful ones. Consider these questions:

1. Is the spirit of home evening the same as what shows up in other family activities? Do I bring my heart to home evening, prepared to link my testimony of the gospel with the events of the day or week? Or do I see home evening as a task that an exhausted parent can barely struggle through? After Church, as a child, I looked forward to visiting relatives for Sunday dinner. Backward turned chairs at the kitchen table greeted us. As we knelt in prayer, we rested our folded arms on those chairs. No more humble reminder of a belief in God could be offered than by those chairs and the willingness of family members to kneel. Small daily moments that precede home evening may contribute to the spirit that's so essential to a lesson. Even incompetently delivered lessons can be offered and received in a generous spirit. Our moments (before home

evening) of soft conversation, or earnest seeking of help from our children, teach what matters to us in gospel truth, and why our family members and home evenings matter to us. The people kneeling at those chairs in Idaho meant more to me than the chairs, but the willingness to pray without considering it a burden infected the spirit of conversation.

2. Do I insist I am a victim of how my children misbehave when they undermine my efforts? If so, I indeed am seeing myself as a victim instead of as the moral agent I claim to believe I am. I discovered that the challenges of farm life, just as the challenges of home evening, could be met with exasperation or compassion. Whether the problem was the irrigation dam eroding or two pre-schoolers pinching each other during the opening hymn, the key to success was not in the difficulty, but in the spirit of our response to it. Farmers who spent time blaming children for setting up the irrigation water wrong, or who became harsh with children over giggling during FHE, didn't solve the long-term problem. The resentment of the harshly treated children lingered in both cases, and thus a tradition of hostile silence infected everything (even, I suspect, the Spirit with which I might kneel for a prayer at a backwards-facing chair). Before we can successfully deliver a home evening, it may be necessary to reconsider our ways.

3. Is it possible that maintaining a quality way of relating to each other (with faith, hope, and charity) is both the purpose and source of successful family home evenings? Some students recalled the qualities of people who had influenced them. Answers included: kindness, patience, honesty, showed love even when I disappointed them, showed confidence in me when I felt a failure, taught me even when I refused to be taught, willing to serve me. The person of influence wasn't perfect, but had qualities that mattered across time, and showed up in everyday life—including home evening.

Alan Osmond, *a member of the former family musical group, The Osmonds, is renowned for performing, composing, producing, directing, writing, and publishing. Alan and his wife Suzanne have a series of children's books about the Next Generation classic fairy tale families, and they write articles and advice in response to questions from families at The Family.com, which is a part of Osmond.net. In the year 2000, Alan received the Dorothy Corwin Spirit of Life Award from the National Multiple Sclerosis Society. He also started a non-profit foundation (OneHeart.org) several years ago, to help strengthen families worldwide.*

★ ★ Family Award ★ ★

EVER SINCE I CAN REMEMBER, OUR FAMILY always had family home evenings. With eight brothers and one sister, we were very close and enjoyed being together. After our mother fixed a special home cooked dinner every Friday night (before the Church suggested Mondays), Father and Mother gathered us around and we visited, played games, laughed, and sometimes wrestled on the carpet. We listened to Mother play her saxophone, and then the piano, with Father singing and us all joining him. That is how the Osmond Brothers started in the entertainment business.

My wife, Suzanne, also grew up having family nights, so we knew how important family home evening could be and promised to have our own with our children. And we still do! Even though most of our kids are married with children and have their own family nights, we all get together once a month at our home. Suzanne fixes a great meal, and we have the best time with our eight sons, their wives, and fifteen grandkids (and counting). We pray together, have a short lesson to strengthen our families and help us be prepared, then discuss goals and challenges. We have games and present our rotating family award (a small trophy) to whoever wins the Family Night Games that month. The trophy really gets around! It keeps things fun, and allows all the family to participate. Nights like these keep our family together and united.

I recently turned fifty-nine years old, and had just returned from the Osmond Family 50th Anniversary World Tour with my brothers and sister, so Suzanne and I got our families together and had a special family night/birthday party. After being away and around the world for six-plus weeks, we shared souvenirs, stories, and pictures—and laughed at memories of funny experiences.

I told my children I was retiring from my travels with my brothers and now want to be a professional grandpa (Papa) with my wife, Suzanne (Mimi). We all shared goals, talked about good times and bad times, job changes, moving into new homes, new babies coming, upcoming recitals, graduations, and ball games scheduled. We adjusted our calendars and made sure everyone was informed. That week, Tyler organized his Eagle Scout Court of Honor. (All eight of our sons are now Eagle Scouts.)

Family home evening is also a great time to face life's tests. I remind my family that a *test* is the first part of the word *testimony!* Having MS has taught me many lessons, and I share how I faced the test and now have a stronger testimony, knowing prayers are heard and that Heavenly Father guides us.

We believe in family night. It is a sacred family time. There is no better way to keep our marriages and families strong and prepared to face these challenging times. The family is God's Plan of Life. We believe in the Church's "The Family: A Proclamation to the World" and feel that family home evening is an important way of strengthening families.

Amy Osmond *(PhD, a.b.d.), the daughter of Wayne Osmond and his wife, Kathy, is a mass media instructor at Arizona State University. She has published articles relating to social justice, online teaching, and critical rhetoric and has presented at academic conferences on subjects relating to critical rhetoric, multimodal rhetoric, and symbolic science.*

Amy has toured and performed for multiple years with the Osmond Brothers. A professional studio and solo violinist, she released her debut album, Nativity *(a collection of traditional Christmas songs performed on the violin and harp), in 2004.*

★ ★ Little Angels? ★ ★

TIME FOR FAMILY NIGHT!" MOM CALLED OUT. All five of us ran to the white couch in the family room and sat there waiting like little angels.

We weren't little angels. In fact, the cushion on the white couch that we were sitting on was turned upside down because my brother Greg had drawn all over it with thick blue marker. And coming when Mom called us the first time? Other than for home evening, that almost never happened. Mom wore herself out trying to get us to come in from playing outside. She finally gave up and got a boat horn—and her ample use of it became the talk of our neighborhood posse. Whenever Mom blew the horn, which could be heard to the end of the block, neighborhood friends snickered and said, "Your mom's calling you!" We had no choice but to go home. Our relative obedience was mostly due to Mom's genius, not our angelic natures.

But on family night, Mom only had to tell us once. We ran to the couch facing the fireplace and waited as Dad and Mom brought out the assignment chart. Our singing time was a pretty interesting endeavor. Mom taught us to lead the music, and Dad taught us how to sing harmonies. He always took the bass part, and Steve, Greg, Sarah, Michelle, and I tried to imitate him. Some harmonies were better than others. Mom told us Steve had a loud voice because he had a big mouth, and he utilized the volume to the best of his ability. I tried to keep up, determined that although I didn't have a big mouth, I could be a big singer.

Dad and Mom wanted to make sure we understood all the gospel principles, so our lessons centered on the chapters found in *Gospel Principles*. Sometimes we had flannel board stories, sometimes object lessons, and sometimes lectures. Occasionally, we got in trouble for giving Mom a bad time. Dad would sit on the edge of the fireplace with tears in his eyes and say, "What have I done wrong as a parent that my children would treat their mother this way?" When time-outs didn't work, that always did the trick.

As an adult with children of my own, I sometimes get lazy and wonder if we can skip holding family home evening—just this week. I have lots of excuses: the kids are tired, the lesson isn't prepared, my husband isn't home from work yet. But then I think how lessons learned as a child helped my testimony grow. I get off the couch, contemplate buying a boat horn, and call my children to family night. Surprisingly, I only have to call once.

Katie Parker *is an award-winning author who writes introspective fiction enjoyed by all ages and faiths. Her book,* Just the Way You Are, *is the first of many.*

★ ★ Flexible Sharing ★ ★

ONE THING I LEARNED FROM MY PARENTS about family home evening was the importance of being flexible. Sometimes you just have to do whatever works.

My dad was a college professor and usually scheduled to teach Monday night classes. So family home evening on Monday evenings was out of the question. Instead, over the years our family home evenings migrated from one evening to another, depending on when family members were available. At one point, we ran out of evenings during the week, so we started having "family home mornings" on Saturdays.

Such flexibility also taught me that family home evening was important enough to make time for, regardless of what had to be done to ensure it happened. You don't have to wait until the perfect time and conditions arrive. They won't. You can make your family home evenings something that works for your family alone. No other family will have family home evenings exactly like yours.

My most vivid childhood memories of our family times together aren't of specific lessons or lectures. The best times were when we simply enjoyed being all together, like the time our TV was broken so we put on puppet shows for each other. Or when we played Monopoly with our dad, knowing we could never beat him but enjoying the game anyway. Or when we all had breakfast together for our refreshments during family home morning. These memories are a part of the tapestry of my family.

When I was in college, the LDS singles would gather at the institute building for family home evening every Monday night. We took turns presenting lessons and leading activities, and responsibility for refreshments rotated as well. Family night there was always lots of fun, and it brought our group of singles closer together as friends and as a cohesive group of Latter-day Saint students on what could be a rather hostile campus.

One memorable occasion, my LDS dorm mates and I performed a skit for home evening. During the course of our preparations, we started openly chatting among ourselves about costumes and lines, and intrigued several of our friends of other faiths. We ended up with four of them coming with us to watch me take on the role of Fred the Hillbilly, one of the other girls acting as the tree Fred tells his troubles to, and the third girl slinging boxes at us from offstage. We ended the skit with our testimonies.

We learned over the course of our freshman year that it was actually quite easy to bring friends with us to family home evening. Bored college students faced with an evening of being locked in their dorm rooms or staring at the walls of the dorm lobby often jumped at the chance to join us for something fun.

Sam Payne, *a celebrated musician, has played on stages from West Coast Universities to the Kennedy Center in Washington D.C. A full-time seminary teacher from 1995 to 2006, Sam now writes books for elementary students, hosts a radio show, and has recorded a popular catalog of original music. His most recent album is* Father to Son, *a collection of songs and stories recorded for a live audience.*

★ ★ Scriptures and Service ★ ★

I REMEMBER COMING HOME AFTER WORK ONE night to a dark house. The boys were in the living room, and Kris, my wife, was not there. I asked what was going on, and they told me that they were waiting for instructions from Mom. It was family home evening. I had no idea what to expect, but sat down and waited with them. Then we heard a whistle from the backyard. We bundled out the door and down the stairs. It was autumn, and already dark, but there was an odd light coming from around the corner—from the stand of trees on the east side of the house. We headed toward it. When we rounded the corner, there was Kris—lit up by two or three halogen work lights set among the trees. She was dressed in a long, white robe (a nightgown from her closet), and she stood on a tall kitchen chair that made my five-foot-four-inch spouse look seven feet tall. The kids were in awe. I was in something akin to awe myself.

Approximating an angelic visit from her perch on the kitchen chair, Kris spoke to the kids about the miracle of the Book of Mormon—which we had just finished reading as a family for the first time—and reminded them of the amazing manner in which it came into the hands of the Prophet Joseph. She pointed to a garden shovel against the brick wall of the house, and invited the kids to dig beneath the magnolia tree. They went to work. A few inches down, wrapped in watertight plastic, they found a package. Inside the package were three sets of scriptures, each engraved with the name of one of our boys.

I'm so thankful for Kris' great desire to instill in the boys a love for the holy scriptures. My oldest is almost fifteen now, and carries that treasured set of scriptures to his teachers quorum meetings and to seminary. He stays up late reading them in his room. The younger boys likewise treasure their scriptures. I don't think they'll ever forget the family night they got them.

We try to include family night service outings some months. The boys grumble at times as we head out the door, but they never come home grumbling. We've often lived among elderly neighbors who have seen and participated in the town's history. Through our home evening service projects, our boys have come to count those people among their close friends. You can't buy that. Not for a million bucks.

While it's certainly not the only place gospel teaching happens in a family, we have found family night to be one of the best places. If the teaching characteristic of family home evening never happens, then the Lord has a lot less to work with when a child needs a potent memory of a gospel principle.

That's partly how we see family home evening: a chance to equip our children with doctrine, feelings, and memories that the Lord can help them access later. Frankly, family night is sometimes fraught with distractions that make it tough to know for sure whether the teaching is making an immediate impact. But there's not one in our family (including Kris and I) that can't cite a time when the Lord, in a time of need, has brought to his or her mind an image, song, or piece of counsel that was shared in some long-ago family home evening—often from an evening when we feared no one was paying attention.

Carol Lynn Pearson *is an American poet, author, screenwriter, and playwright. She is known for her book* Goodbye, I Love You *and the LDS musical* My Turn On Earth. *Her play* Facing East, *about a Mormon family dealing with the suicide of a gay son, opened Off Broadway on May 29, 2007. Carol Lynn also wrote* One on the Seesaw, *a lighthearted book about raising a family as a single parent.*

★ ★ The Christmas Light Thief ★ ★

A S THE VERY BUSY SINGLE MOTHER OF four busy children, my stabs at family home evening were sometimes pathetic. I remember going down the hall and calling, "Family Home Five Minutes! Time for Family Home Five Minutes!" Sometimes that seemed the only way to get in something that qualified as a bit of focused sharing.

But occasionally we managed more than that. Frequently the more successful family home evenings were prompted by a particular event that required handling. Such as the time Brent, a neighbor boy, stole our outside Christmas lights. Emily, then twelve, sleuthed out the offender's identity and marched up to his house, banged on the door, and said to his mother, "Brent stole our Christmas lights, and I want them back right this minute!" She came home triumphant with a paper bag full of our lights.

I devoted our next family home evening to discussing what Jesus told us to do about Brent.

"Huh? Emily got the lights back. What else? Call the police?"

"Actually, Jesus told us to do something else."

"Like what?"

"Like—love our enemies."

"Love Brent?"

"Return good for evil. Do good to those who steal your Christmas lights."

"Good? Like what?"

We talked about it being pretty obvious that Brent needed more light in his life. Otherwise, he wouldn't have done what he did. Maybe we should . . . give him some light.

"Like how?"

"Well, what if we give him a secret gift?"

After a spirited discussion that went from scorn to interest to excitement, we decided to gather up our pennies and buy a flashlight and wrap it with a note that had Brent's name on it and leave it on his porch. Aaron, our fastest runner, won the privilege of delivering our gift.

Now, many years later, in spite of the many family home evenings that never happened or were botched, I have reason to believe that my children recall an occasional hands-on lesson on a subject like "Do good to those who steal your Christmas lights."

Lisa J. Peck *is a Certified Relationship Coach through the Growth Climate organization. She has built an award winning film and book business, and has eighteen books written to date, including the CTR series,* Escaping the Shadows, *and the Mothers of the Prophets series. Lisa is also the former host of the radio program, "The Hero Factor."*

★ ★ Role Playing ★ ★

ALTHOUGH WE HOLD FAMILY HOME EVENING WEEKLY, they are never too complicated because our family is large and our schedules hectic.

One favorite is when we open with prayer, pick a hymn relating to something with which we are having difficulty, and discuss the concepts contained in the words of the song and in the scriptural references at the bottom of the page. Sometimes I choose, since I usually know what we need, but other times another family member decides what needs singing about.

Our younger children often beg to prepare a different kind of lesson—maybe something they've learned at Church, or at school. They find all the necessary material, then present to the rest of us.

Perhaps our most successful FHEs are when we role-play the how-to-deal and how-not-to-deal with certain situations. For example, if a child is undergoing bullying at school, we'll play it both ways, and discover various coping skills. The child learns to interface with others in a non-offensive way in a safe environment, and my husband and I get to see what's going on in our children's lives.

Marvin Perkins *co-authored with Darius Gray (October 2007) the groundbreaking set of DVDs entitled* Blacks in the Scriptures *that details the biblical and LDS doctrine on people of color, skin color, curses, and the priesthood.*

Marvin, *a recipient of the 2004 Humanitarian award by the National Council of Community and Justice, is also an accomplished vocal recording artist, and currently serves as cochair for Genesis Public Affairs. He has represented the Church on numerous television and radio programs, and served as Director of African American Relations on the Southern California Public Affairs Council.*

★ ★ Learning Manners ★ ★

IN OUR HOME, THE CALL OF, "GIRLS, it's time for family home evening," is usually followed by two little girls running and screaming with excitement. Asia and Milan love family night. At the ages of three and six, the girls need the event to be fun in order to get the lesson across. So my wife, Ani, and I take turns coming up with creative ideas to solidify this as a tradition the girls will carry on when they begin their own families.

Whatever the lesson, home evening for us always begins the same way, with a prayer and then a song—or two. Ani and I never get to sing. Our daughters will either make up a song, or sing one of their favorites, complete with impromptu choreography. If my wife and I are strong, we can keep it to one song and move on to the lesson.

One lesson format (below), which has become a family favorite, is where we teach the girls manners and social skills. We decide on a principle and then act out "the wrong way" followed by "the right way." We often end up with each of us on the floor laughing hysterically.

★ How to move past someone in a public or private setting: I start out demonstrating the wrong way. And will move past each of my participants bumping and nudging them out of my way with a few other antics added in. After we compose ourselves,

I then show the right way by politely saying excuse me and then waiting for the others to acknowledge me before moving past. Each family member gets a chance to demonstrate both ways.

★ How to respond to someone who says something that is unkind: I start out by demonstrating the wrong way. Ani says something to me that makes me unhappy. I then respond with something that has the girls rolling on the floor laughing. Then we do it again, only this time I respond in a way that either validates what I perceive to be the concern in Mom's statement, or one that defuses a potential conflict. Again, everyone gets a turn to do both, and we generally have so much fun with this one that we have to cut if off from going too long.

Before heading to the kitchen for treats, we end each lesson with a scripture that ties the message of the lesson together. A fitting passage for the above lessons:

Yea, and are willing to mourn with those that mourn; yea, and comfort those that stand in need of comfort, and to stand as witnesses of God at all times and in all things, and in all places that ye may be in, even until death, that ye may be redeemed of God, and be numbered with those of the first resurrection, that ye may have eternal life. (Mosiah 18:9)

Dr. Grant Pitman *is Superintendent of Police responsible for the Communications Branch of the Queensland, Australia Police Service. He has over thirty-years experience in operational and support functions of policing. While employed by the Queensland Police Service, Grant completed a PhD and authored over thirty academic articles and book chapters. He is a retired Stake President, currently serving as the Multi-stake Director of Public Affairs for Queensland.*

★ ★ Pitmans Are One ★ ★

OVER THIRTY YEARS AGO, MY WIFE, DONNA, and I made a decision to hold family home evening on Monday nights. Our six children have enjoyed participating in these nights ever since. When my law enforcement duties and university studies sometimes required me to work on Monday nights, the family made another night available.

Family home evening has varied over the years depending on the age of our children and changing demands placed on our family. We sometimes had family friends participate, often resulting in them hearing the gospel of Jesus Christ.

One particular home evening had a significant impact on the way the Pitman Family operates. My wife and I had read the Stephen Covey book entitled *The Seven Habits of Highly Effective Families* and decided our family needed a family mission statement and a brand name. We explained to our children the purpose of a mission statement based on both church and family values, and discussed an appropriate brand name.

After many ideas, including a suggestion based on the movie, *The Mighty Ducks,* the family name became "Pitmans Are One." The family purpose or mission was that all family members would be invited to attend (and where possible, support) all activities, family service projects, and significant Church events, such as ordinations and baptisms. The children suggested this mission statement be included in annual family goals, and visually recorded for all to see. We decided to have T-shirts made with the Pitman brand name embroidered on them.

Extended family saw the T-shirt displayed at family camps and activities, and this resulted in other Pitman families adopting their own brand names. Our grandchildren now wear their t-shirts with pride and regularly participate in family activities.

The T-shirts have also given our children opportunities to explain the Pitman way to other people. During a recent family holiday at the beach, a person approached our children asking about the brand name on the T-shirt, which he thought was a business name. The children explained what the name meant and how it applied to our family and church values.

As family members continue to value and practice our mission statement at home evenings, and wear family T-shirts at all Pitman activities, the Pitman way continues through generations.

Dan Potter *is a motivational speaker who presents "Nice It Up" workshops at BYU's Especially for Youth, and also works with major companies throughout the U.S. Dan's six children, The Potter Kids, are members of the Screen Actors' Guild.*

Home Evenings on a ★ ★ Grand Scale ★ ★

I WAS TRAVELLING WITH BRACKEN JOHNSON (BULLY from the Napoleon Dynamite movie), addressing schools in California about being a VNP (Very Nice Person), when it struck me that these kids, who were having such a hard time being nice to each other, really needed family home evening. Because there was rarely a parent at home, they never learned decent behavior from anyone other than each other, or actors on TV and in videos. So I took home evening to them on a grand scale, and taught them lessons my wife and I gave to our own children.

Organizing family night was hard in our home. Our six children were active in the entertainment industry, auditioning and shooting between studies in a home schooling program. But we knew the importance of FHE and were determined to hold it. Meaningful gospel discussions happened about once a month, sliding in between fun activities—little teaching opportunities from us as parents or from older siblings that wouldn't have happened any other way. President Kimball called these, "Golden threads of testimony." The children didn't realize they were being taught.

I often wondered whether family night accomplished much. Recently, however, on receiving a call from a grandchild telling me it was her turn to conduct home evening, it hit me. This had gone through a generation. And when our grown children tell me how much they enjoyed earlier FHEs, I feel joy. Our children love each other and remain in close contact to this day. How sad if, at this stage in our life, we could only say, "We wish we'd held home evenings."

Dr. Craig Raeside *is a medical doctor and forensic psychiatrist in South Australia. He is responsible for providing psychiatric services to prisoners, victims, and the courts, and gives expert evidence about the interaction between mental illness and criminal behavior, as well as the effects of substance abuse, gambling, and other destructive behaviors. He is a regular contributor in the local media about mental health issues, drug and alcohol disorders, and offending. Dr. Raeside is also a Major in the Australian Army Reserve and has served as a Stake President in Australia for ten years.*

★ ★ The Bedrock of a Stable Society ★ ★

FAMILY HOME EVENINGS HAVE BEEN A CENTRAL part of the unity and love our family has experienced over the years. But is has not always been easy. Lesley and I married soon after I returned from my mission to Italy after which I resumed medical school. By the time I graduated, we had two young boys and a third child on the way. Although studying full time and working part time seemed a challenge when holding regular family nights with our young children, it was nothing compared to what awaited in the working world!

As a medical officer in the Australian Army following hospital residency, I was often required to work Monday nights. We decided that rather than not hold home evening, we would have a main FHE on Sunday afternoons and some type of activity on Monday nights even if I was not home. Later, during my training as a psychiatrist, I again worked long hours. Persistence and flexibility were the keys. Lesley held things together and sometimes all I did was preside!

As with other families, our five children were not always perfect during home evening. There always seemed to be one who wanted to wear the "Let's-be-stupid-during-home-evening hat." We tried to be flexible, while also catering for the ten-year age span between our eldest and youngest child. Just when we thought we'd worked things out, they became teenagers, with a number of different challenges, including a variety of different schedules, interests, attention spans, and temperaments.

Now, working as a forensic psychiatrist involved in the assessment and treatment of mentally ill criminal offenders, I see all aspects of life. My testimony that each person is a son or daughter of God, and that family life and righteous parenting are at the bedrock of a stable society and emotional health and wellbeing, has been strengthened. Given these experiences, we had some interesting discussions in family home evening about Church standards and the teachings of the prophets. I was able to share my first hand experience about people who chose to live differently and the consequences of those choices.

From our own experience with nearly thirty years of trying, struggling, and keeping at family home evening, we found the following helpful:

1. Stay focused on the family as the highest priority in life amongst all the other demands.
2. Make a commitment to hold regular, weekly, meaningful home evenings.
3. Be organized, but flexible, in what to do and when to do it.
4. Parents should work as a team, lending support to each other with a common purpose. Identify the family's needs and plan accordingly.
5. Don't give up. Persistence is essential despite things that seem to get in the way.

We discovered increased blessings of family unity and love; balance between family, church, and work; and the opportunity for our children to learn from us and hear our testimonies in their own home.

Tom Roulstone *is an author who was born in Donegal, Ireland, and moved to Glasgow, Scotland before emigrating to Canada. His first novels,* One Against the Wilderness, Fleeing Babylon, *and* Home to Wyoming, *were followed by his Passage of Promise Series:* Elisabeth, Inheritance, *and* Last Wish.

★ ★ Tape It for Posterity ★ ★

WHEN MY LATE WIFE BETSY AND I raised our six children, we tried to have family home evening regularly. As I think back to those days, all the Monday nights coalesce into one. However, several years after Betsy passed away at the age of forty-three, I was going through some things and found an audio-cassette recording of a Christmas home evening. Each family member had contributed something relating to Christmas: one read a poem, another played the piano, another told a story, and so forth. Tears came as I listened to my children and wife. I am so glad we made that recording, and recommend the practice for special home evenings.

Now that my new wife Serenity and I are empty nesters, our family home evenings are much less structured. Recently, we invited a couple, William and Sandra, from our ward to supper. After we ate, we went out in our canoe (we live by a lake) and Serenity taught the lesson. She began by giving us twenty questions to come up with an "element of nature." After fifteen questions, we finally realized that we were floating on it: water! Then Serenity asked us to recall as many scriptural incidents, parables, and so on that involved water. We were surprised at just how many there were from the Flood, to the baptism of Jesus, to Jesus' encounter with the woman at the well. Afterwards, we continued our discussion as we ate a delicious Chilean (Sandra's from Chile) desert. All in all, it was a wonderful evening with the right mix of temporal and spiritual.

Linda Keilbart Scanlan *has won numerous poetry awards and was nominated by the International Society of Poets as the "New Poet of the Year for 2004." Her children's book* ONE *sells to an international market. She is also a contributor in the book* Forged in the Refiner's Fire *and is a disabled Navy war veteran.*

★ ★ Lessons for Life ★ ★

THREE FAMILY HOME EVENING LESSONS STAND OUT in my mind. The first was a lesson on enduring to the end. My thirteen-year-old niece was living with us. She was heading in the wrong direction fast. I wanted to teach her that although it wasn't easy to do what was right all the time, it was worth it, not only for this life, but in the eternities. She understood the concept of enduring to the end, but had no basis for the principle. A week later, she had a massive pimple on her forehead that was causing her much pain. After a few days, she asked if I would take care of it. The pimple was large and stubborn. As she pushed against my fingers she was nearly in tears even though the head was about to pop. I simply told her to endure to the end just a little bit more. She learned what the principle meant and fifteen years later, she still repeats the story.

The second story is about my twin girls who were seniors in high school. The home evening lesson, based on the *My Turn on Earth* song "Choosing," taught that the first step on the road away from the iron rod was not necessarily wrong. Not going to school one day wasn't wrong, but if a person continues down that path they might end up a delinquent. Dating a non-member wasn't wrong, but you may never have a temple marriage. The Holy Ghost would whisper to us when we started down a road that was not conducive to the Lord's will. If we listened, we would be safe. The twins decided to skip school several months after this lesson. Both girls were with boys we would rather them not be around. Smoking and drinking was involved in this wayward adventure. One daughter realized where she was heading and immediately decided she didn't want to live like that the rest of her life. She married a returned missionary in the Vernal Temple. Her sister never caught on to what was happening. She didn't marry in the temple and her children know nothing about the Church. The difference is apparent in their countenances, physical health, and emotional well-being.

In the third story, the children returned from school and I told them we were expecting some very important, special guests for home evening. The house needed to be ready to receive them. I prepared special refreshments of vegetable trays, chips, cinnamon rolls, and various other treats. The table was set with a tablecloth and our good dishes.

The living room was being cleaned when our elders quorum president dropped by. He said hello and made sure we were fine, then left. I told the kids that although he was important, he was not our special guest. As we continued cleaning, the bishop and his wife stopped by to check on us. Again, I explained to the children that although they were important too, they were not the special guests. The fervor increased as the furniture was vacuumed and the shelves dusted. A member of our stake presidency then stopped by prior to going on a date with his wife. The kids expected him to be the special guest and again I said he wasn't.

Finally, the house was clean and I made a big production of looking out the window and saying "They're here!" The kids went running outside to see who this very special guest was. They didn't see anyone and asked who it was. I said it was them. They were the ones who were worthy of the fine treats and movie we would be watching. The little one's eyes lit up and ran inside to begin their feast. The oldest one, however, realized that Mom had a clean house!

Lee Ann Setzer *has several published books for children such as* Tiny Talks, *the Sariah McDuff series, and* I Am Ready for Baptism; *and an adult story*—Gathered: A Novel of Ruth.

★ ★ The Adverb Singing Home Evening ★ ★

ONE OF OUR FAMILY'S FAVORITE FAMILY NIGHT activities is something we call "Adverb Home Evening." One reason we like it is that it can be adapted to any size, any age family.

1. Get out the hymnbook.
2. Open to page 1, or any page you like.
3. Look at the upper left of any hymn, near the top. There should be an adverb there: "resolutely," "reverently," "cheerfully," and so on.
4. Now that you know where to look, page through the hymnbook, reading the adverbs. Soon you'll have a whole list of positive, but very different adverbs. Notice that they tend to cluster—a whole set of "resolutely," "firmly," "diligently," followed by the "happily," and so on.
5. Sing your favorite hymns. Try to make them sound like the specified adverb.
6. Now, think about yourself. Which of the adverbs describe you? Do many of them describe you, but at different times? Is it "better" to live "cheerfully" or "reverently"? Or are Heavenly Father's children as varied and wonderful as the songs of Zion? Which adverbs would you like to incorporate more of into your life?
7. Have refreshments. Symphony bars?

Paul B. Skousen, *father of ten, is the author of* The Skousen Book of Mormon World Records *(and the sequel), and* Brother Paul's Mormon Bathroom Reader. *He is a former intelligence advisor in the Reagan Administration and has been a journalist and a communications professional for most of his adult life.*

★ ★ Good Words? ★ ★

STREAKING THE PROPHET IS NOT A NORMAL agenda item for family home evening, but for a three-and-a-half year old, some fifty years ago, the act was not an attempt to destroy Monday night—it was just showing off. And technically speaking, Ezra Taft Benson was not the prophet.

My little brother Brent and I were bored. We slipped out of the bathtub and scurried to mom and dad's bedroom where we huddled, shivering, to plot our surprise race through the living room. President and Sister Benson, along with Brother and Sister LeGrand Richards, were visiting my parents. Their conversation was rich with hand gesturing and doctrinal linkages to worries of the time. At the peak of some spellbinding profundity by my dad, Brent and I burst in, full sprint, giggling and screaming, racing within arm's reach of that shocked group of adults before Mom could scoop up Brent, grab me by the hand, and lead us back to the tub. I still remember the look on Sister Benson's face. Her jaw dropped about as far as powdered skin can stretch. As for the three dads, well, they just kept talking.

Thirty years later, I was on the receiving end of such a surprise. Kathy's folks were visiting for home evening. I was ready to show off my four faultless children, all under the age of six, and demonstrate how well we had made the gospel the central focus of our lives. That particular night, I gave the "Good Words Lesson." I placed on the floor a pile of sweepings from the kitchen. Into the mix, I put favorite toys. I explained there are many words in our world, some good words that we keep, other bad words, like the garbage, that we throw away. I invited our children to pick out the good "words" by removing their toys. That's when I made the point. "And just like this trash left behind, it is the same with bad words. We should throw them away." I scooped up the trash, poising the dustpan over the wastebasket. Then I made my big mistake. I asked, "Kids, what are some words we should throw away?"

From those little innocent mouths came such eloquence, such mastery of the phraseology, syntax, and locution as they rehearsed back all seven of the forbidden utterances yet conceived by the vulgar mouth of man. Aside from my face turning beet red and the ticking of the mantle clock, I sensed a sucking sound as if air in the room was drawing out. There I knelt on the floor, hand frozen over the wastebasket, slowly letting the tokens of a backfired message hush their way into the bin, and my little angels looking up at wise dad for some acceptance that they had done their darling best. I glanced over at my mother-in-law. She looked just like Sister Benson.

Regardless of the struggle or boredom that sometimes takes over in home evenings, we are gratified with one constant ending that wraps up our time together. Toward the end of the lesson, a question is posed, or memory triggered, and everybody visits in friendly, animated exchange. Family home evening becomes just that for us, half an hour that lengthens, ultimately filling the evening—a warm, memorable time of trust and sharing, free of criticism and judgment.

Today, Kathy and I prepare to visit distant cities, sit in on our children's home evenings, and check that the gospel is being taught to their children, just as we taught ours. And we secretly hope none of them will try out the "Good Words Lesson."

Lu Ann Brobst Staheli, *2008 Best of State Educator K-12, is a former Utah English Language Arts Teacher of the Year, Nebo Reading Teacher of the Year, Christa McAuliffe Fellow, and past president of both the League of Utah Writers and the Utah Council of Teachers of English. Lu Ann is the co-author of* When Hearts Conjoin, *the story of Kendra and Maliyah Herrin, www.utahtwins.com.*

Using Family Night to Make
★ ★ a Family ★ ★

I SUPPOSE YOU MIGHT SAY MY FAMILY is a little unconventional. None of us are blood relatives, and only my husband has been a member of the Church all his life. The rest of us are converts and adoptees. I first learned about the Church and converted in college. My children were adopted from the foster care system when they were three, five, six, ten, and thirteen. None of them had ever lived in an active LDS family, so suddenly my husband and I were full-time missionaries, doing all we could to teach each of the boys what we believed, while we were learning how to be parents and examples at the same time.

The first two boys were easy. They had at least attended a church before, although teaching them not to refer to Jesus as "Papa God" caused a couple of embarrassing moments in those first few weeks. Soon they were both involved in Primary and happy to listen during family home evening.

The others were a little more complex. The youngest was only three, so listening during family time was a challenge. The ten-year-old was a people pleaser, but sometimes he tried to please the wrong people. That's where the oldest boy stepped in. It was his job to make sure we weren't teaching his brothers anything he deemed as crazy, and just about anything that came out of our mouths fit that description in his opinion. Right when we were about to give up on teaching those two the gospel, they demanded to see the missionaries. So, for the next several weeks, we had wonderful family home evening lessons, taught by the elders.

Five years have now passed, everyone is a baptized member of the Church, and some weeks family home evening goes well, and others it doesn't. On occasion, family night ends with everyone being sent to his room for the rest of the evening. We may not be perfect, and my husband and I are certainly still learning about better parenting, but at least we are trying.

If there is anything I've learned about having a successful family home evening, it's that the best laid plans of mice and men . . . No, wait! That was someone else's idea. Anyway, always prepare for the unexpected. If a kid can think it, he will be sure to say it, and the things a set of boys think can make you blush or just plain go crazy.

Some of the best lessons are Open Question and Random Scripture nights. With Open Question night, the boys can ask anything on their mind—and they do ask anything. We've had discussions about school, missions, movies, books, cars, girls, and even sex. Moments of embarrassment aside, all this talk has left us closer and the kids understand they can come to us with anything. Random Scripture night also leads to great discussions. Someone calls out a book, chapter, and verse. Sometimes we know ahead of time what it's about, and others we have no idea. We read the scripture aloud then discuss awhile before moving on to the next suggested scripture. It's amazing how much these boys can get out of a single verse, and it's also interesting how sometimes these random calls seem to follow a topic or theme.

So, maybe our best family home evening lessons aren't very formal, maybe they aren't so conventional, but with an unconventional family like ours, why would we ever expect it to be?

Three members *of the Suleymanova family,* **Elena, Artur,** *and* **Diana,** *from Siberia, Russia, are renowned in their community. Artur is star forward on Irkutsk's professional soccer team, and Branch President of the local LDS Church; Elena is an award-winning soprano soloist and music academy teacher (her choir won the Children's Choir Festival in Bulgaria in 2007) who sang duet at the Helsinki Finland Temple dedication, 2006; and Diana has countless music and dance awards.*

★ ★ Teaching the Missionaries ★ ★

I N OUR HOME, WE LOVE SHARING OUR talents with others, especially in family home evening. Once, we invited our local missionaries, and instead of them teaching us, we taught them. My mother (Elena) showed the missionaries how to conduct music. First, she taught them how to conduct two/four, then three/four, and then four/four. It was fun watching the elders learn the techniques of conducting. Some elders did it very well. This is also a great family activity.

Sometimes we invite members of the church, or missionaries who have musical talents, to our home evenings, and we have a little home orchestra. Mom plays the piano, I play saxophone, someone else plays guitar, and we sing different songs and hymns. Whenever we have these unusual home evenings, Dad takes a video camera and records what we're doing. This makes good memories for us and for future generations.

Sometimes, it's hard finding time for home evening because we are all away from home about eighteen hours a day. But when we do find time, we feel so blessed, and it strengthens us, and our testimony of the eternal family and of the gospel.

Bruce Summerhays *was inducted in the University of Utah Athletic Hall of Fame in 1998. Among his many golfing accomplishments are two PGA Senior Tour wins—in 1997 at the St. Luke's Classic, and in 1998 at the State Farm Senior Classic. In 1996, he earned the PGA Senior Tour "Ironman" title. Bruce coached golf for two years at Stanford and was named PAC-8 Coach of the Year. He designed three of Utah's golf courses, including the Homestead in Midway.*

★ ★ Pushing Past the Obstacles ★ ★

WHEN MY WIFE AND I WERE FIRST parents, we had no clue how to rear a child. We had a keen sense of responsibility and deep desire to do it properly. While studying the scriptures, we came upon 1 Nephi 15:24, "And I said unto them that it was the word of God; and whoso would hearken unto the word of God, and would hold fast unto it, they would never perish; neither could *the temptations and the fiery darts of the adversary overpower them* unto blindness, to lead them away to destruction" (italics added). This answer to our prayers made us determined to hold weekly family home evenings and teach our little ones the gospel, thus providing protection from the fiery darts. We weren't perfect, of course. Sometimes, when the children were ornery and fighting, and it seemed like we should quit home evening that night, we pushed ourselves to have it anyway, and often experienced the most spiritual lessons in the end. It was obvious someone did not want us to have those lessons.

There were many more Monday night obstacles, such as school events, little league, or dance recitals—even friends who came over because their own lesson was finished, or took place on Sunday, didn't help. We wanted family home evening, not family home half hour or lesson.

Having more children than the standard assignments, we added our own categories, the favorites being the "joke" or the "yell." The yell went like this: I would say "It's time forrrrrrrrrrrrrr . . ." and they would reply, "Faaaaaaaaamily, home eeeeeeeevennnnnnnning!" followed by the song "This is the Night We've Waited For." My daughter, Susanna, realized only recently that we didn't make up the song after seeing it in the children's hymn book.

Looking back, the children had two favorite FHEs. The first, when my wife Carolyn was expecting our eighth child and I came home to a real mess. For the lesson that night, I tied a book to the front of each child's tummy, and then a pillow on top of the book to imitate being pregnant. Then I asked them to pick up all of their toys. They cried, whined, and said it was so hard, but eventually got the point of how tough it was for their mom to clean up after them with a baby in her tummy.

The next lesson we still laugh about today happened in the early eighties and all our children were still home. I threaded a string around the yard and through the house. It was quite an obstacle course. Then I blindfolded the children and had them hold on to the string (rod) and follow it to the end. I talked them through it as they went. The first lesson learned was that they were embarrassed to be outside where their friends could see. The concept of the great and spacious building became real to them. Then their unique personalities came out. One son, who was always relaxed, was playing with his yo-yo. The yo-yo-string tangled with the rod string and he started following the wrong one. We all saw how easy it was to get off track. The others talked him back to the real string. In the end, everyone cheered each other on to the finish. We found parallels depicted by the lesson for a long time afterward.

Cameron Taylor *is the author of* Does Your Bag Have Holes? 24 Truths That Lead to Financial and Spiritual Freedom. *He is the president of four organizations—three for-profit companies and one educational charity—and received the Circle of Honor Award for being an "exceptional example of honor, integrity, and commitment."*

Teaching With Analogies
★ ★ and Games ★ ★

WE HAVE TWO YOUNG CHILDREN AGES FIVE and two, so my wife and I incorporate object lessons and activities into our short lessons. For one of the lessons I was giving on the role of the Spirit to testify of truth, I blindfolded my wife and two children, put a jellybean in each of their hands, and asked them to say what flavor it was by feeling it with their fingers. Then I asked them to put the beans in their mouths and tell me the flavor. It wasn't until they internalized the bean that they knew the truth. I asked my children if they could tell if the scriptures were true by feeling them and, of course, they answered no. I used this analogy to explain that as we read the scriptures and internalize them, the Spirit can then testify of the truth to us.

Another popular FHE in our home is scripture Jenga. My wife or I tape scripture references (or quotes on a topic) to Jenga blocks and we play a game of Jenga. If the Jenga piece pulled has a paper taped on it, we read the quote or scripture, discuss it, and then continue with the game. The use of games, analogies and object lessons have been very helpful in keeping our children's attention and they look forward to the lessons, often asking if we can repeat the same games, stories, and object lessons.

We did a joint home evening with my wife's sister's family and the children really had a good time. I taught the lesson from Proverbs

13:20, which reads, "He that walketh with wise men shall be wise: but a companion of fools shall be destroyed."

I shared the following story from the life of Christopher Columbus: After Columbus discovered -the Americas, he was invited to a banquet where he was assigned a place of honor at the table. He was served with ceremonials normally reserved for kings. From across the table, a shallow courtier, a man who was jealous of Columbus, asked, "If you had not discovered the Americas, would there not have been other men in Spain who would have been capable of the enterprise?" Columbus made no reply but took an egg and invited the company to make it stand on end. They all attempted the task unsuccessfully and lamented that it was impossible. He then struck the egg upon the table so as to break one end and left it standing on the broken part, illustrating that once he had shown the way to the new world, nothing was easier than to follow it. Following someone who has achieved what you want to achieve is the simplest and quickest way to get where you want to be.

I asked the question, "Who are some wise men today that we can follow?" The answer came back, "The prophet and apostles." I replied, "Yes. They show us the way to happiness and eternal life. We simply have to follow their counsel, advice, and direction."

Following this lesson, we divided into two groups to re-enact a story from the scriptures. Our group chose the story of Ammon cutting off the arms of Lamanites in defense of the king's sheep. We all had a part to play. A blue blanket served as the place of water and a star wars light saber served as Ammon's sword. We filmed the re-enactment and watched it together. It was entertaining watching the young children crawling around and baaing like sheep as I tried to gather them after they were scattered. The kids enjoyed seeing themselves on film, and it also created a memory and recording of a wonderful time spent together as a family.

Vickey Pahnke Taylor *is a song-writer/producer, vocalist, and professional speaker, and has performed and/or taught in numerous venues. Her compositions include the theme songs for the Special Olympics program (state-by-state selection), the Make A Wish Foundation, the Especially For Youth program of the Church, and the Families In Focus program. She is a Billboard award winning songwriter, with hundreds of songs to her credit.*

★ ★ He Who Laughs, Lasts ★ ★

"HE WHO LAUGHS, LASTS"—THANKS TO THE AUTHOR of that thought. Around our house, if you can't exercise your sense of humor, family home evening—or anything else—is going to be a bust.

From early years, thinking all too naively that well-thought out and prepared lessons would be appreciated and anticipated by the children, to many years later as worn and wiser parents, we've found that laughs are the thread that tie our home evenings together.

Trying to teach principles that matter to smaller children in a church-like setting does not work at our house. I remember one child whose favorite trick was to roll from the back of the couch onto the couch itself, and then somersault onto the floor . . . repeatedly. Or he would start giggling and not be able to stop. Of course, the other kids joined in. Then there were the times of asking, begging, bribing, and warning as they performed new and exciting (note sarcasm) antics.

The long and short of it is this: I finally got it through my head that maybe I was approaching family night in the wrong manner—at least for my family. Because I had been focusing on the lesson or the principle, I had missed the fun! The very core of spending time together was slipping away from us.

So—we started laughing. I learned that the lessons should be very short and/or very interactive. Instead of focusing on a principle that we must explore, we began focusing on a principle we could casually touch on, while we were having fun together. Soon enough, family home evening became more fun—and it was easier to get the point across.

Then, and now, we could calm down long enough for the prayers and the hymn. Sometimes we had a night when the stars aligned, and an actual lesson and more detailed conversation evolved. As we look back, the thing that bound it all together best for us was the laughter. Believe it or not, humor became the glue that allowed a principle to stick!

For families with young children, teenagers, or whatever the circumstances—enjoy the time together. Creating happy, fun times together is important. Beautiful lessons can be carefully interwoven—ever so sneakily—with humor. And the memories we make are grand.

Laugh!

Carole Thayne *is the author of two published books,* A Question of Trust *and* False Pretenses. *She is also a potter and has exhibited and sold her work in galleries and art festivals throughout the West.*

★ ★ Hunting for Meaning ★ ★

ONE FAMILY HOME EVENING THAT STANDS OUT for me was when our daughter was nineteen and our son newly married. It was the first year our daughter-in-law participated in our annual Easter egg hunt—an occasion when we found a beautiful place in the canyons near our home and my husband hid candy-filled plastic eggs.

During an earlier Relief Society Enrichment night, our teacher told the Easter story with symbols and thoughts. As she went through the story, she opened plastic eggs one at a time. At the end, the last egg was empty symbolizing the empty tomb and that Christ had risen. She had also prepared for each of us our own set of eggs and symbols. I included these in our canyon home evening hunt.

My husband went ahead of us and found a hillside fresh with new growth and the smells of spring. He hid the symbolic eggs and the candy-filled eggs. Our daughter-in-law was excited since she hadn't done many hunts before. On the count, we all started running and gathering eggs, each with a bag in hand. Our daughter, seasoned by years of egg hunts quickly gathered eggs, three or four times more than the rest of us. Then we sat together on a blanket, divided the eggs, and, using the numbered eggs, told the Easter story about the Atonement and Resurrection. It was a beautiful reminder of the real meaning of Easter.

Dian Thomas *has over thirty years media experience and is a nationally renowned TV personality, professional speaker, and author of twelve innovative books, including the New York Times best seller,* Roughing It Easy. *With over five thousand television and radio appearances, including* The Tonight Show with Johnny Carson, *many more on* Good Morning America, *and eight years on NBC's* Today Show, *she is dubbed "America's First Lady of Creativity."*

★ ★ Home Evening Cooking ★ ★

MY FATHER WAS A FOREST RANGER, SO our family grew up on outdoor fun, all the way from family home evening to family outings. We discovered one of the best ways to create family memories was cooking together outdoors. I remember my dad cooking sour dough biscuits in the Dutch oven when I was about ten. I fell in love with outdoor cooking. Those early experiences lead me to a spectacular career in teaching millions the secrets of outdoor living.

When I was young, there was not a designated time for family home evening but we were always encouraged to do things as a family. The memories I enjoy today of family activities together, include milking the cow and getting the cream so that we could all help Mother make cream puffs. Another time, we all helped Mother build a canvas (in the days before plastic) swimming pool, in which we had numerous swims as a family—until my brother played Tarzan and flew into the pool and out the other side.

The memory-making aspect of cooking together as a family happens when each member becomes involved in making his or her own dinner or desert. Not only is this easier on the parents, but the children have a real learning experience that stays with them for life. The following dishes were winners in our family, and a great treat for a special family home evening.

Foil Dinner for Four

★ 18-inch heavy-duty aluminum foil
★ 2 carrots, peeled and thinly sliced
★ 2 medium potatoes, peeled and thinly sliced
★ 2 onions, sliced
★ 1 pound ground beef, shaped into four patties (or chicken, or fish)
★ 1 teaspoon salt
★ ½ teaspoon pepper

Cut four squares of foil. Divide vegetables into four equal portions. Layer with one-half carrots, potatoes, onions, and ground beef; finish with onions, potatoes and carrots in that order. Season with salt and pepper. Seal by folding down in small 1/2-inch folds until package can no longer be folded. Flatten the two sides of the package, then roll the open edges toward the center in small folds. If the package needs wrapping again for strength, place the folded top of the package upside down in the center of another piece of foil and repeat. Cook on a bed of hot coals for 15 minutes on each side. Serve as a main dish or supper. Serves four.

Banana Boat

★ 18-inch heavy-duty aluminum foil
★ 1 banana, unpeeled
★ Miniature marshmallows
★ Milk chocolate chips or broken candy bars

Cut a slit lengthwise about two-thirds of the way through the banana from the stem to the base. Fill the slit with miniature marshmallows and milk chocolate chips or broken pieces of chocolate bars. To heat the banana boat, wrap in foil and cook on hot coals for five minutes, or until the chocolate and marshmallows have melted. If you leave the boats in the coals too long, the bananas will liquefy. Serve as a dessert or a treat around the campfire.

Francesca Torcasio *lives in Italy and is the author of* Domus Aura, *a book on spirituality and home keeping; and co-author of* Motorino— I Love You, *a book on motorcycle riding safety for teenagers. She is also a renowned artist of many popular paintings, including* The Son of Man, *and* The Laughing Girls.

★ ★ Clean Home, Clean World ★ ★

My problem was keeping our teenagers' bedrooms and bathroom clean. Being unable to solve this problem was frustrating. Even the visit of friends and parents wouldn't motivate the children to clean up the mess and make their rooms presentable.

One day, as we walked in the woods, our kids commented on the beer bottles and other items littering the path side. They couldn't accept the idea that people would just throw these things in the woods and be so careless about keeping nature unpolluted. We talked about safeguarding the environment and about the value of clean water. We considered how badly we hurt Mother Nature when we litter the woods or the fields with every sort of garbage, leaving a negative legacy for future generations.

That gave me an idea. The next morning I returned and took some pictures of the litter we had noticed the day before. Then I went home and photographed the items that littered their rooms—the clothes on the floor, the paper cups. This time they were directly involved, and there would be no blaming others.

I printed the pictures and prepared some visual aids for our family home evening. I started by talking about the environment and showed pictures of a clean forest, then our path in the woods with the bottles and cans. "The environment is a gift to us all," I suggested. "Not only for those who live nearby, but for visitors and guests as well." They all agreed. Then I showed the pictures of their rooms, with all their disorder and items left around.

I explained that home is the place where the family lives together, where we welcome guests, friends, and relatives. It is not respectful toward others, family members or not, to live in a messy room. Then I showed pictures of the house with clean rooms, flowers and a flood of light coming through open windows. I asked them what emotions they felt when looking at the two sets of pictures. Of course, the difference was clear. Just like the woods, our house needed to be cared for and protected.

Things did not change miraculously the next day, but that family home evening did help our children see things from a different viewpoint. They began taking responsibility for their part of the home environment, and became aware that they could indeed contribute to making our world a better place in which to live. They also realized that this way of thinking needed to begin at home.

Arch J. Turvey, *from England, served as President of both Birmingham and Romford Stakes following which he was called as Regional Representative for the London, England Area. He retired as Area Manager for Guardian Royal Exchange Assurance to serve as President of the England London Mission and later served with his wife, Olive, as President and Matron of England London Temple.*

★ ★ From the Perspective of Time ★ ★

MY WIFE AND I LED FULL LIVES, both from the aspect of many callings, and from making our family time rich by building love for each other. Looking back, two pictures flash to mind—family holidays we shared, and the time we spent in family home evenings.

We have two sons born eight years apart, which might seem difficult if home evenings were just reflecting on Gospel messages, but we made it work. When both boys were at home, we began with a brief, spiritual message assigned to each of us in turn. Then followed a fun game of football. We were fortunate in having a large hall available so weather didn't matter. The younger son and I were always on one side while the older son played against us, watched by my wife. Invariably the older son won, and sometimes his brother ended up in tears, protesting at some real or imagined infringement of the rules. Mention those soccer games today and each will recall those happy, fun times. Refreshments followed—ice cream or sweets—anything to make our outing happy and united—the words *happy* and *united* being the goal.

Later, when the older son married, we continued with assignments, although the message was more sophisticated and refreshments more elaborate—and we moved on from football to squash. We rejoiced when our younger son always kept Monday evening free for family night, even when he discovered girls.

Family holidays were closely associated with family home evenings because they were also times shared together, not because we should, but because the experience was joyful and something to which we all looked forward. Our sons now have families of their own, and they too have the ongoing goal of sharing time with family.

My counsel is as follows:

1. After prayer, spend a little time to plan.
2. Include something whereby even the smallest can have a little input worthy of praise.
3. Don't be too rigid—have some fun time.
4. Remember, the goal is not to have family home evening for itself, but to develop love for each other, which, if achieved, means so very much and will automatically achieve many goals.

Console yourselves that if at first you don't succeed, you're like most other people. Don't give up!

GG Vandagriff *is a writer of genealogical mysteries, suspense and historical novels, as well as non-fiction. She also writes a twice-monthly column for Meridian Magazine. GG has many titles to her name, including* The Arthurian Omen *and* Tangled Roots. *Her latest books are* Deliverance from Depression: Finding Hope Through the Power of the Atonement, *and* The Last Waltz.

Around the World with
★ ★ Home Evening ★ ★

OUR CHILDREN'S FAVORITE HOME EVENINGS WERE WHEN we pretended to visit different countries. We set up the bathroom like an airplane and my son was the pilot. After we arrived at our destination, we had dinner featuring selections from that particular country's cuisine. Then we had a missionary who had been there show his slides. It gave the children a great opportunity to see the world outside our little Midwestern town and to know the church existed all over the world.

Sometimes the very best thing about having family night is simply the tradition. One of our children was struggling with a very difficult problem, which he brought up at the end of home evening when he was certain of our attention and certain the Spirit would be there. We had been clueless. Because of that family home evening, we were able to get him the help he needed.

From a very young age, our children loved sharing responsibility for family night because it gave them everyone's attention. They were always very creative and feel they owe their strong testimonies to family home evening experiences, family prayer, father's interviews, and goal setting.

Jeff Wright's *words have appeared in the Church News and Ensign Magazine. He has written several opinion editorials, including a contribution published in* Americans on Politics, Policy, and Pop Culture: The 101 Best Opinion Editorials from OpEds.com (2005). *Jeff contributes regularly to professional publications writing articles on leadership, planning and performance management. He is an internal consultant for the U.S. Coast Guard.*

★ ★ Invite Him Home ★ ★

AS A SINGLE ADULT MY THOUGHTS AND experiences relating to family home evening are in many ways unique. Earlier years in the Utah Valley gave me opportunities to participate in single adult home evening groups, which were plentiful and quite active. In my singles ward, efforts were made to give us some of the same experiences as families. Often, our Monday night would start by meeting at the church and hearing a message taken from a Church-published family night resource manual. We then piled into cars and headed to an activity—like the time we went to the park and played a team version of Frisbee; or when we invaded a movie theater; or the times we simply went out for ice cream (the counter people at the Baskin-Robins just loved seeing our group coming).

For one particular home evening activity sticks out. I lived in Salt Lake, and the previous Sunday, the focus was on the sacrifice made by pioneers. On Monday evening, we loaded into cars and drove to a nearby ski resort. It was summer and the activity was to take the lift to the top and hike back down. It did not take us long to realize that even going well off the beaten path to find a more gentle slope, we still had to switch back in order to progress down the mountain. As we walked, one of our leaders reminded us of the pioneer lesson and that we were traversing terrain very much like the pioneers did, only many of them were pulling handcarts. Just then, one of the sisters started singing the primary song "Pioneer Children Sang as They Walked." We all joined in and had a memorable evening.

Other family home evening's we would stay at church and have a powerful gospel lesson/discussion, similar to lessons received on Sunday, but the weeknight atmosphere prompted even more questions and discussion. During most of those intense family night discussions, I learned more from my surrogate FHE family than I did from our instructor. The singles home evening group, while spiritual, leaned heavily to the social, and I had a personal rule that I would not date a girl until after we had met and talked at a family night or Sunday evening ward prayer.

When I found myself outside the Utah environment, home evening, as I knew it, virtually ceased. My activities now fell on me to plan and execute. Most often they would be extra alone time reading scriptures or church magazines. Sometimes I would treat myself to a movie or even a special meal. The best experiences were invitations into a member home on Monday evening and participating in family home evening with a loving family. I remember one large family in particular. In time, we built a relationship, and eventually invitations were not just for family night, but Sunday dinner; or a service opportunity helping with a project at their home; or to watching General Conference. I will never forget the December Monday evening when this family invited me to dress as Santa Claus and visit with the children. Being a younger single adult, without a Santa body structure, this was awkward for me, but when I sat down with that family, it turned out to be a very happy occasion and resulted in what I imagine was a more memorable home evening for Santa than it was for the children.

Margaret Blair Young *is the wife and former student of Bruce Young. Both teach in BYU's English department. Margaret is the author of five novels (three co-authored with Darius Gray) and is a frequent award recipient from the Association for Mormon Letters. With Darius Gray, she is also the co-producer/director of the documentary,* Nobody Knows: The Untold Story of Black Mormons. *Bruce Young's book,* Shakespeare and Renaissance Family Life, *is published by Greenwood Press.*

★ ★ The Family Dance ★ ★

M Y HUSBAND, BRUCE, AND I WERE NEVER terribly ambitious with family home evening, but it was important to us, and our four children always enjoyed at least part of it: the refreshments. Our FHEs always began with the Family Dance, which comprised of raucous jumping, gymnastics, or arm waving, accompanied by a polka-esque song Bruce composed years ago. Of course, as our children approached their teen years, doing the Family Dance was far beneath them— though our married daughter has loved to see her own children dance to Bruce's music. When she married, I gave her a kit to make her own FHE chart and a cassette recording of Bruce Young's inimitable Family Dance.

In the early years of our marriage, I made a family home evening chart of a little wooden house (two-dimensional) and moveable hearts bearing each family member's name. The hearts would move from window to window, each window designating an assignment: prayer, music, scripture, lesson, activity, refreshments. Though some children approached their assignments with more enthusiasm than others, family home evening became a time we all enjoyed. The one assigned to "activity" often chose a night of bowling or (more rarely) a movie. We loved playing "In the Manner of the Adverb," where one person leaves the room while the others choose an adverb like "timidly" or "crazily." When the person returns, he or she asks the others to perform various tasks "in the manner of the adverb." "Shake my hand in the manner of the adverb." "Give me a hug in the manner of the adverb," and so on.

Perhaps the most memorable home evenings were spent with Bruce's sister, who was in a care center suffering from M.S., which had paralyzed her. She was unable to speak but, until the last months of her life, was able to smile. She always smiled when we brought family home evening to her. And after visiting her, we visited others in the care center as well, even if only to sing a song. One resident, Cookie, had been our neighbor. Bruce was once her home teacher, though she told him she had no intention of ever being active in the Church and didn't want his visits. He found ways of keeping in touch with her nonetheless, and soon she eagerly anticipated his visits. When we visited her in the care center, she accepted hugs and kisses from our children, and often had candy or cookies for them. She did finally go to church there—perhaps prodded by the promise of the branch president that he would do a jig in front of everyone if she came. She did, and he did.

Whenever we pass the care center now, I think back to the years it was such a big, vital part of our lives, and particularly part of our home evenings. I think those evenings we took to the care center were the sweetest of all, and the ones I remember with the deepest affection.

The last time our grandchildren visited for family night, Bruce had to think hard to remember how to play his Family Dance composition. We never transcribed it, and he hadn't played it for years. After a couple of false starts, it finally came back to him. We all danced like children—at least in our hearts.

About the Author

Anne Bradshaw, who was born in Wales, grew up in England and now lives in the United States. She has authored three published books, including *Please, No Zits! & Other Short Stories* for LDS youth. A feature screenplay she co-authored won first place (fantasy/sci-fi genre) in the International Family Film Festival—Hollywood, CA—and was a Finalist in the Action on Film International Film Festival. Anne has also written countless magazine and Internet articles, and has a blog at www.annebradshaw.blogspot.com.